# ESCAPING INSANITY

*Secrets of the Covert Narcissistic Psychopath Exposed*

**silence of the narcs**

Disclaimer

The information presented is the author's opinion and does not constitute any health or medical advice. The content of this book is for informational purposes only and is not intended to diagnose, treat, cure, or prevent any condition or disease.

Please seek advice from your healthcare provider for your personal health concerns prior to taking healthcare advice from this book.

ISBN: 9798848395938

# Contents

## Dedication

I dedicate this book to my youngest daughter and my father, who gave me purpose and were my rock during some of my darkest days, to my close friends, for their time and lifting me up when I was down, the survivors who shared their journey and knowledge about abusive people and to my faithful dogs and horse who gave me unconditional love and devotion through all the years.

**#NOCONTACT**

**@silenceofthenarcs**

**silence of the narcs**

# Introduction

Have you ever woken up one day and wondered who the person lying next to you in bed is? Or maybe some days your spouse is the same person as the one you married on your wedding day, but other days they are entirely different with no explanation as to why? Have you ever found yourself frustrated and lost in your relationship? Then, when you attempt to bring up your concerns, you're told it's *you* that's the problem. Perhaps you've lived your whole life devoted to your partner and your family only to have the rug swept from beneath your feet as the lifestyle you've grown so accustomed to is ripped away.

Suppose any of the above situations resonate with you. In that case, you may be in a relationship with a narcissist, or worse, a covert narcissistic psychopath (CNP), the most dangerous kind of them all. Maybe you've heard the word narcissist floating around before but have never given it much thought. Your partner is perfect; everyone loves them. How could they be a narcissist? Yet something isn't right, and being around them winds you up indescribably until you find yourself exploding left and right. That is how my relationship with my CNP ex-husband went, and I wish I'd known about covert narcissism before I lost twenty-seven years of my life. I'm writing this book not only to bring awareness to covert, narcissistic, and psychopathic personality disorder but also to share my story in hopes of helping others heal from their own toxic relationships.

To start, we shall dive into my past and how I got involved with a CNP. I joined the dating scene later than most in my young adult years. At the tender age of eighteen, having had no other serious relationships, I met my first boyfriend in college. My only other dating experience had been a 2-week trial with a boy in eighth grade. Peer pressure and the feeling of flattery that someone was interested in me led me to give the boy a chance. I was neither emotionally nor physically interested in dating or in him, but at the same time, I wanted to know what it would be like to have a boyfriend. Our brief relationship ended swiftly, for he had what many teenage boys have on their minds: sex. He was more interested in necking and getting with as many girls as possible, while I desired an emotional connection.

My first real boyfriend was fairly handsome and a skilled martial artist. All the students in my Karate dojo looked up to him, for he was quite the character. Though he made me laugh and flirted with me, he never dared to ask me out. We traveled to many tournaments together, winning first in both Kata (forms) and sparring (fighting), placing us amongst the top competitors in our club. In contrast to my home life, where nothing could ever please my critical mom, I felt on top of the world while competing in martial arts.

Don't get me wrong, I love my mom, and she had a good heart, but I was a constant failure in her eyes. Sadly, neither of my parents was all that interested in my activities. My father worked hard to support our family. We didn't come from money, and my parents had been through war, loss of family, and the deaths of their own parents. Their harsh childhoods molded them into strong individuals, which I greatly admire. And yet, they never let their past hardships interfere with my brother's and my childhood, for which I am grateful. However, from my youth on, my mom would describe me as over-sensitive. I agreed with her as I frequently felt overwhelming empathy and emotions within.

Growing up, my female influence, my mom, followed the role of raising the children while my father worked. From watching my mom, I was taught that women are there to serve their husbands, raise their children, and tend to the household chores while men work, spend some time with their family during meals, then go back to work. My father was very respectful and loving towards my mom. Though I am not denouncing my mother's choice in any way, my conditioning growing up as well as the false narratives society often presents to young girls, paved the way to my slipping into the trap of a covert, narcissistic psychopath. Furthermore, childhood films of princess fairytales and gender roles modeled a fantasy of an idyllic relationship. As I grew older, it became evident relationships required equal commitment and hard work from both parties.

My first relationship was my most memorable, for the bad moments were nothing compared to my second relationship and eventual marriage. He was a strapping, young blonde with blue eyes (which was my weakness). We were a year or less apart, unlike my ex-husband, who was nine years older than me. From the beginning, I couldn't truly be myself as he was sensitive and didn't understand sarcasm. And because I cared deeply for him, I didn't want to hurt his feelings by saying the wrong thing. We started dating after a year of knowing each other at the martial arts club and after several away tournaments together. After arriving home from a successful tournament, we celebrated by going on a trip to the beautiful sandy, white beaches of Caramel by the Sea. I can vividly remember it as one of the happiest days and trips of my life. Young, new love is an enchanting feeling. I wish we could bottle such affection. Around him, I was giddy; we played chase in the sand, and he swooped me up into his arms. Before I knew it, our romance had begun.

However, the euphoria of a new relationship didn't last. His insecurities throughout our time together developed a year and a half into the relationship. I didn't understand why he felt insecure about us. Instead of letting me know directly and talking out his concerns, he became spiteful, acted with the intention to hurt, and his jealousy grew uncontrollably. He'd get upset if any other guy looked my way while we were out, regardless of whether I saw or acknowledged the guy. After minor encounters, he would ghost me for a week or two. I let him have what I thought was his cool-off time. Only when I'd receive the mean letters he wrote and left on my car would I know what upset him.

The letters contained made-up blame, false accusations, swearing, name-calling, and utter brashness. They confused me. How could he bear such a false impression of me? How could he call me such vulgar names? What did I do to make him feel this way? The winds felt taken out of my sails. I hadn't done anything he'd accused me of. After all, I can't control others looking my way, nor did I dress in a suggestive manner. In fact, my attire was conservative to the point my own mother asked me when I would enter a convent to become a nun.

It reached the point where simply hanging out with other girlfriends or working longer resulted in more ghosting and letters. I felt suffocated, realizing nothing I did could make him see I wasn't the villain. Eventually, I had to make one of the hardest decisions at that time and let him go. It was rough on both of us. We tried to make it work once more, but in a few months, he was back to his old jealous antics. A male friend of mine, who happened to be gay, came to my twenty-first birthday party thrown by my family. It was a simple gathering of close friends and family. I wasn't much into large parties like my family was. Rather, I enjoyed quaint celebrations with those who meant the most to me.

When I arrived at the restaurant, I spotted all my friends, but I was mainly looking for him. However, he was nowhere to be seen. My friends and family were all having a good time, and when I asked if they knew where my boyfriend was, they said he was invited but did not come nor let them know why. The letter arrived on my car, like usual, a few days later, graphically accusing me of cheating with my work friend. He said he hoped his "fat ass" didn't crush me! It was utterly preposterous, and his shameful prose disgusted me. Not only was my friend obviously not into me that way, but I hadn't slept with my own boyfriend, let alone any other man. At that time, I held old-fashioned values and wanted to wait until marriage. I couldn't fathom why he would accuse me of something so opposing to my nature.

The fact my first love could write such filth and falsehoods on my twenty-first birthday, a day that should have been filled with joy, was the last straw. Though my family and friends surrounded me, I had never felt so unloved as my boyfriend chose to be jealous of something he'd conjured up in his mind. I didn't know what narcissism was back then, but I knew something was not right within him. Though his behavior was toxic, his actions were more overt. He never said we were "soulmates" or love-bombed me as a CNP does. However, this behavior was my first experience with what is called a dating "Red Flag."

You will learn about red flags and what to look for, but first, let me define what a Covert Narcissistic Psychopath is. My first boyfriend was not in this category. Overtly narcissistic individuals are much easier to recognize and protect yourself from. Although their behavior makes no sense and is hurtful, you can still see it coming. Typically, you can see that problems in the relationship are with the overt narcissist, not yourself. With a covert narcissist, you are led to believe you are the only one creating issues. The covert narcissist can do no wrong in their own eyes, and it isn't easy to pinpoint precisely what feels off.

## Covert, Narcissistic, Psychopath Defined

The technical definitions as defined in the Merriam-Webster dictionary are as follows:

Covert – not openly shown, engaged in, or avowed.

Narcissistic – of, relating to or characterized by narcissism: such as

A: extremely self-centered with an exaggerated sense of self-importance: marked by or characteristic of excessive admiration of or infatuation with oneself

B: displaying or marked by excessive concern with one's physical appearance

**Sociopath**: a person with a personality disorder manifesting itself in extreme antisocial attitudes and behavior and a lack of conscience.

**Psychopath**: very charming, manipulative, and controlling, who behaves dangerously or violently towards other people and does not feel guilty about such behavior.

The difference between a sociopath and a psychopath must be noted to understand the personality of a CNP better. Many assume psychopaths are violently dangerous individuals that seek to murder and physically torture. However, that is not the case. In fact, as with every mental challenge, there is a spectrum. There are violent psychopaths and sociopaths at the higher end of the spectrum, but at the lower end, there are the ones that can assimilate into everyday life, though their actions still hurt other individuals. However, the hurt is not deadly or physical.

Psychopaths lack a conscience and tend to be more manipulative than sociopaths. They are deceptively charming and more likely to lead a normal life without acting on any desire to kill. When it comes to their criminal activities, psychopaths try to minimize the risk of exposure, not keen on getting caught. Contrastingly, sociopaths are not as manipulative and are more prone to behave impulsively or act on their rage. Unlike psychopaths, they cannot maintain a standard work and family life. Sociopaths don't bother hiding their true selves, content to make it known that they do not care how anyone feels.

I will discuss the covert, narcissistic psychopath personality type in this book to shed light on the dangers of these emotionally abusive individuals. CNPs are the silent killers, the ones who slowly suck the life from you with invisible hands. They can destroy a life or, in the worst case, take a life, using covert manipulation.

For years I was gaslighted, mentally and physically abused, and entirely blindsided. Eventually, I became a person I could not recognize. I was stressed, sad, explosive, and reactive. Everything wrong in my marriage was somehow my fault. My husband was the angel while I was the crazy one. After an exhausting two-and-a-half-year-long, draining divorce, I began to see the light of my marriage - or should I say fraud marriage, unmarriage, or "matriphony," not matrimony - more clearly.

Within the divorce and discovery, all his secrets unraveled before my eyes. It was a complete shock to my already compromised psyche. Truth be told, when I first heard the word narcissist, I couldn't see how it applied to my ex-husband. I thought of the typical cinematic narcissist, someone outspoken, loud, or egotistical. Someone that treated others as if they were beneath them.

That didn't entirely sound like my husband. There were moments where he seemed caring. Then, he would morph and take on a new, vindictive form, becoming unrecognizable. Yet, his behavior was blamed on me. He took no accountability, for he could do no wrong. That's when I further researched narcissism and discovered something far worse than the typical narcissist we find easy to hate.

The Covert Narcissist is a living Dr. Jekyll and Mr. Hyde creature. A Covert Narcissist is ultimately more dangerous than the Overt Narcissist. We see the Overt for who they are. They're rude to our face and prefer to go straight for the jugular. However, the Covert Narcissist prefers a quieter method. Think of it like the story of Hansel and Gretel. Coverts spread a little breadcrumb path of care or "love," leading you to that house of confections. But little do you know... evil awaits inside. Then, when you leave the nightmarish house coated in sweets, the breadcrumbs are gone until the next time the Covert Narcissist wishes to entrap you.

Once I learned the traits of a Covert Narcissist, things began to add up. I could match my ex-husband to the personality disorder and am still, to this day, amazed at how it explains everything. However, some things still did not fit the nefariousness of his actions. I did some more digging and learned about the psychopathic side of covert narcissism. Suddenly, everything fit into place. How he seemed to enjoy my pain, and his inability to care about others had confused me. His apathetic behavior, followed by outbursts of anger, left my mind spinning. A lack of genuine connection was covered up by lies that held me captive, hoping it would get better again soon. Unfortunately, I hung on for too long as that "soon" never came.

I wish to share my experience with a covert, psychopathic narcissist while helping you notice the red flags, realize the signs, and ultimately escape the cage that is living with a narcissist. In this book, I hope to shed light on a new level of narcissism, one of the most abhorrent. The CNP drains you of happiness, self-worth, and the will to live. Though I carry no background in psychology, the story of my life with a CNP has given me more than enough knowledge to know what and who to avoid in the future. I'm going to share what I've learned with you in hopes of preventing more victims of narcissistic abuse.

Through my story, I hope, dear reader, that you will gain valuable insight into the relationships in your life and be able to distinguish between a healthy individual and a toxic individual. One of the most valued principles I've learned is that of "No Contact." We will discuss this concept further in the book, but it is of the utmost importance. Should you be in a relationship with or encounter a CNP, the way to rid yourself of their malicious presence is to stop all communications with them. There are myriads of ways a covert, narcissistic psychopath will attempt to draw you back in, but in this book, I will teach you how to push back.

The path to freedom may appear daunting initially, but the end result will be liberating. The truths I reveal in this book may be shocking as well as disturbing but will lead you to the path of healing and growth. Now, turn the page, and let's begin the journey.

# Chapter 1: Red Flags

The first time I met my ex-husband, let's call him X for short, should've been the last time I saw him. I was coming off a three-year relationship, missing having a companion or partner to do things with. One of my childhood friends invited me out to meet some of his friends. I wanted to meet new people, so I agreed and was later introduced to X. Although I wasn't aware of it, X was with his current girlfriend whilst flirting with me.

We'd shared a common interest in the martial arts and had the same Kubaton keychain. I had also competed at his club's Tae Kwon Do tournaments without knowing he was there. Only when we arrived at the movie theater did I discover he had a girlfriend. She was visibly upset throughout the movie and ended up leaving halfway through, sobbing. X's excuse was that she didn't like the movie. To me, that had seemed like a valid excuse. Little did I know, I had just missed two red flags.

Now, what exactly are red flags? Red flags are warning signs that something is amiss or dangerous. The first red flag was his expression of interest in me while he had a girlfriend. Though he hadn't tried anything yet, he made no indication that he had a girlfriend. That type of red flag is easy to miss, especially if you are unaware of the relationship status of another person. However, when it becomes clear to you a person is in a relationship but they seem flirtatious or overly friendly, a hint of unfaithfulness can be seen. This red flag was small, barely visible. However, it did not remain small; you will see what I mean later in the chapter.

The next red flag was the behavior of his girlfriend. First, she was sobbing during a movie that was neither sad nor dark in nature. Looking back at the situation, his excuse that she was crying because she didn't like the movie did not quite fit the atmosphere. Something else must have been amiss. Most likely, it was X's doing. Still, I missed the red flag. I took him at his word and looked past the occurrence. Looking back at that memory, I am still shocked at how I fell for such a weak cover-up. The movie was not something to cry over, but the abuse from X certainly was.

Later in the evening, we returned to my friend's place, and I conversed with X about martial arts, specifically self-defense. This conversation drew me to him as he seemed rather knowledgeable. Intelligence was something I'd been attracted to. X portrayed himself as a very bright individual, well above others. He had knowledge of things I didn't know about. I'd asked him what-self-defense techniques he practiced, and he offered to show me.

Curious, I agreed. X's movements were quick and rough, putting me into a choke hold first. Initially, I thought it was weird that he was acting so physically, but my competitive spirit propelled me to continue and not tap out just yet. However, X was bigger and stronger, performing a defense move in which his finger pushed up on the apex of my nose hard. A burst of pain shot through my nose, and I raised my hand, tapping out immediately. I was shocked and confused, not expecting X to hurt me. I'd thought he would demonstrate the defensive techniques, not utilize them. My hand went up to my sore nose, which felt as though it might be broken. I was angry and bewildered that a man could do this to a woman, especially one he barely knew.

This had to be one of the biggest red flags of all. Here was a man I'd just met who'd physically hurt me. In fact, I'd gotten a large bruise from the encounter. When I exclaimed how it had hurt, all he'd replied with was, "then it was effective." Later, his friends nonchalantly claimed he didn't know his strength or had just lost control. But violent men don't lose control. After all, they don't lose control and beat their boss or someone bigger than them. They don't lose control in public or in front of family. When a man hurts you, no matter how angry he may seem, they are in total control of themselves and you.

Looking back at this now, I wish I'd run the other way and never given him a second thought. However, CNPs are good at getting you to do something you don't want to while making it seem like it was your decision. I was very attracted to intelligent men, and the way he held himself portrayed the idea that he was a man of great intellect. His friends all believed he was brilliant as well, which affirmed his wisdom greater in my mind. After all, they would know, for they were closest to him.

I hadn't stayed connected with X after that night, so I was surprised to receive an invite to his birthday party. I've never been one to turn down free cake, so naturally, I went. Peculiarly, when I arrived at the party, I discovered X wasn't there yet. He was late to his own party. I shrugged at how strange that was and chatted with other people. I momentarily wondered why his girlfriend wasn't there but later found out the pair had broken up, which didn't necessarily surprise me. The tension between them had been evident when they'd last hung, and they'd seemed to be an ill-fitted pair. X had a calmer persona that appeared not to mesh with his ex-girlfriend's more emotional demeanor.

Finally, X arrived at his birthday party, showing the guests his canoe and describing how he maneuvered through the challenging whitewater rapids of a river. I was engrossed in the story, surprised at how such a plain, disheveled-looking man could do such fascinating things. He appeared to be both outgoing and intelligent, traits I valued in any person more than physical appearances, which he certainly lacked.

Towards the end of the party, I fell into conversation with X, eventually feeling comfortable enough to ask about his breakup. He described his ex-girlfriend as someone with extremely low self-esteem and little confidence. He also said she would, and I quote, "bitch, moan, and complain." X claimed that everything with her was an argument that she wanted to get married, and he wasn't ready. He continued, lamenting how she'd suddenly changed her mind when he finally agreed to marry her. X portrayed her as emotionally unstable and incredibly needy.

What made me miss the earlier red flag was how calm, confident, and sane X had sounded compared to his ex-girlfriend. From how he talked about his ex, I could understand why X would want to break things off. Then again, they were much older than me, so perhaps it

14

was the right time for marriage, though I could not imagine wanting to get married so soon.

What I didn't realize at that time was that this was another red flag. One of the most significant clues that someone is a narcissist, covert narcissist, or covert narcissistic psychopath is revealed through how they talk about their exes. Most people avoid talking about their ex, especially on the first date. It's usually painful to talk about, awkward, or too personal for starter conversations. However, narcissists have no problem discussing their previous relationships, especially if it makes them look like victims.

An overt narcissist will make sure you hear loud and clear why their past relationship didn't work out and what their ex did wrong. Coverts go about it differently, especially if they are a CNP. They'll make you feel they are confiding in you and that you should be empathetic to their plight while secretly hinting you should not act as their ex did…or else. CNPs are perpetual victims in everything. They are the ultimate chameleons and blame shifters.

Keep this fundamental truth in mind. All the things the CNP's ex supposedly did are things the CNP did and will do. The way their ex treated them is how *they* actually treated *their* ex. Instead of taking accountability for what they did wrong in their past relationship, the CNP blame-shifts it all onto their ex, and they will do it to you in the discard phase. Blame-shifting is something all narcissists do when confronted. Rather than accepting they are at fault, they throw it back at you, listing everything you did to cause the problem. The blame for the issue is shifted to your side until you apologize for something that was not your fault. In reality, their accusations are confessions or projections of their behavior.

When a relationship with a CNP ends, they will find some way to make it your fault and take note of it. Behind your back, they document everything, including things that happened years prior. This is an especially crucial point to register in your mind because what they are documenting is *your* reaction to *their* abuse. Then, they utilize it as evidence to throw in your face later or to prove you are emotionally unstable. The more you try to defend yourself, the more volatile you appear. It's all a smokescreen used to prove they were victims and had no hand in your emotional reaction to their insidious, crazy-making abuse.

CNPs don't let go nor heal from the slightest constructive criticism. They will never admit their faults, and if they do, it's to further manipulate you or their next target. So, if someone begins smear campaigning their ex on the first date with you or the first time they meet you, recognize that is indeed a red flag.

A smear campaign occurs when the narcissist begins tarnishing your name to whoever will listen, painting you as the villain. It is done to you in secrecy to rob you of the ability to defend yourself. When successful, the people the narcissist smeared you to will believe every word they say, ostracizing you rather than the actual perpetrator.

Maybe you're reading this book to heal from a toxic relationship or think your ex/current partner might be a covert, narcissistic psychopath. Or perhaps you've never heard of that term, but none of the other terms seem to fit that person exactly. Whatever the case, red flags are vital to recognize whether you've left the relationship, remain in the relationship, or wish to pursue one. If you've just ended a relationship, realizing what red flags you missed in the past will help create new connections, not just romantic ones. You can protect yourself better once you recognize the signs of a toxic person, especially a CNP. CNPs are more common than you may think. In fact, you may know many of them without realizing it, as they are exceptional at masking.

Their mentality is similar to, if not exactly like, a cult leader. CNPs learn how to prey on the naïve and master their manipulative techniques from historical cult leaders. X bragged about how he studied cult leaders from an early age, which should have been yet another red flag to me. After all, cult leaders are covert sociopathic or psychopathic narcissists, skilled at promising their victims the world (also known as Future Faking), only to take it away once the victim is firmly under their control.

However, not all CNPs desire to be cult leaders. Other CNPs prefer to entrap one victim to get their supply from rather than a cult following. Nevertheless, they prepare a backup "supply" should their main target start figuring them out.

## Common Red Flags Before You Enter a Relationship

Most CNPs share a variety of common red flags, the most prominent being the digs towards their ex or people they do not like. These are typically subtle but effective.

17

## Love-Bombing

People have the need to be loved and enjoy being complimented and cared for. The desire to hear praise and feel like you are the center of your partner's world is an addicting feeling. But it can also be dangerous. Love-bombing occurs when a person starts showering you with praise, gifts, affection, anything to make you feel as good in their presence as possible. It occurs at the beginning of a relationship and is often over-the-top for such an early stage.

A strong indicator of someone being a CNP is if they tell you they love you or feel a profound affection for you within the first couple of weeks or first month of the relationship. Love-bombing is everything you want to hear but is a tool to make you dependent on the CNP for their affection, allowing them to control and abuse you.

The most harmful part about love-bombing is that because the CNP's idealized version of us lines up with our idealized version of ourselves, we believe they fully see us when, in actuality, they do not. They perceive us solely as a tool to be used.

Love-bombing indicates that the person does not see your true self and pretends to, which is a problem in and of itself. Someone not seeing you for who you are, both positively and negatively, should be a red flag. The CNP may claim they see you, and their idea of you may match up with how you feel about yourself initially, but as they get to know your insecurities, the CNP will tell you a different story later in the relationship.

Rather than bring up your good qualities, they will use your insecurities to put you at fault in the relationship. For example, at the beginning of the relationship, the CNP may compliment how honest and trusting a person you are. But later, they will switch their tone and admonish you for being naïve or immature enough not to believe their point of view.

CNPs use love-bombing to shield their true intentions and keep you blind to any slips of their mask. My first date with X was a disaster, ending in him closing a tow truck door on my finger! However, he told me that my brown eyes were beautiful, something I had never been told before, and that I was his brown-eyed girl (like the song). I had thought that was so romantic then and overlooked how terrible our first date was. This happened a lot in our relationship. X's abusive actions were covered up by honey-sweet words that masked the taste of the real poison underneath.

## The Terrible Texters

Just because someone does not text back immediately or isn't on their phone often, in general, does not make them a CNP. However, it is a red flag if the person constantly uses their phone or has it around them but still ignores your texts. Don't get this confused with a person taking some time to respond because, of course, we are all busy and can't reply right away. With texting, you can usually tell when someone is avoiding texting back, especially if they've texted you back quickly before.

For example, a covert narcissist I worked with had no problem texting back when she was answering a question that suited her. When you disagree with a narcissist, they get "injured." They blow a minor offense out of proportion, acting as though you personally attacked them. When I sent messages that challenged her way of thinking, which was very close-minded, she pretended as if I hadn't sent her a message at all. Only when I asked in person if she'd seen my text message I'd get a response.

She would say that she saw the text but that she needed a couple of days to recover from it as if my text had been considerably offensive. Yet, my text was formatted respectfully when I had a question or if I disagreed with her. It got to the point she barely responded to my texts or emails at all, leaving me off email threads. You were valued as long as you accepted everything she did and agreed with everything she said. Disagree, and you were nothing.

With X, he simply did not reply at all unless it benefitted him. He often strung my daughter and me along. If my daughter asked for something, he would either not reply or just respond with a maybe. Then, after waiting a couple of days, she would ask again, only to get the response that she was pressuring him and acting too much like her mother (as if that were the worst thing she could do). If she played it right, sometimes she could get what she needed, but it came with the price of a guilt trip in the future.

However, he often continued this game of maybe until we gave up or, as he hoped, forgot about it. This tactic keeps them from having to decide or take accountability. By exhausting you to the brink, it's easier for them to simply walk away and forget about it, leaving no blood on their hands. There is no real relationship with these sick individuals because everything is left unresolved and ignored. You are not important enough should your needs not fit into their agenda.

Especially with long-distance, having a relationship with a narcissist that purposefully avoids your texts is exhausting. Teenage girls deal with this problem regularly when it comes to boys. They'll see the boy active on social media, but he doesn't respond back, trying to make himself more desirable if he appears disinterested. These silent treatment games are unnecessary and harmful, yet so normalized. Just because tons of people do something does not make it right. I will discuss the silent treatment in Chapter 2, but it is one of the worst forms of emotional abuse regularly used by CNPs. By allowing yourself to be treated that way, you may not realize you've opened a door for a true CNP to slip through.

When dealing with a CNP, it would be in your best interest to go "No-Contact." I will repeat this term throughout the book, for it is the best way to handle any narcissist. Suppose you feel ignored through text, getting the tiniest scraps to hang on to. Let the person you're texting come to you. Try not to text them for a while, and if they message you, give short replies. You do not have to feel bad about it. You're establishing the boundary that you deserve to be acknowledged. You will find that having self-respect will weed out the toxic people and make room for the healthier ones.

If you can't go completely No Contact, I suggest you use the Grey Rock method. The trick is to become as solid as a rock. Don't react to their abusive neglect, comments, digs, passive aggression, nothing. Be a rock against their storm until you can walk away for good. Address matters that need to be addressed and, if they won't comply, find other solutions. Anytime the CNP tries to rage at you or accuse you of something, feign confusion or essentially "play dumb." Letting the CNP think you are clueless or not as intelligent as them will assuage their egos enough so that some semblance of peace can be achieved and so you can work towards getting free from their control without drawing suspicion.

Reacting to their abuse is quite normal and is a way of trying to cope by expressing your emotions. However, it becomes mentally exhausting, negatively impacts your physical and mental health, and causes further torment. If their words strike you through the heart or their actions frustrate you, you will achieve a better result by not outwardly reacting and won't allow the CNP to tarnish your reputation. When you react emotionally, although your feelings are valid, the CNP twists your behavior and uses it to prove to others that you are out of control or what they consider "crazy."

For me, the amount of neglect towards myself and our kids led me to finally hire help instead of tirelessly pleading with him to put in the effort. We had more than enough money, but X bellyached that *his* precious retirement was being spent. He wasn't worried about our retirement as a couple or his children's college future. X's sole concern was to inflict pain and stress upon others, and he used his money to do so. Not to mention, I knew we had upwards of a million dollars in investments, so his financial concerns were as false as his fraudulent self.

He was unavailable and unreliable. He often forgot to pick the children up from school and didn't make an effort to arrive on time for school or their activities. As long as it meant X could continue being absent, he was willing to hire anyone available without vetting them, as he did not care if our children were put in harm's way. In his care, he often put them in harmful situations, so I made sure to vet each prospect properly. Although we went through many mother's helpers, I found some who eased my worries, were caring, and hardworking.

The caretakers often became another means of triangulation – bringing in a third person as leverage against the victim – encouraging them to take his side or quit. He didn't succeed; ultimately, they could see he was rarely present and disrespectful. Several people, including caretakers through the years, would ask me why I hadn't left him yet. Looking back, I wish I had because staying with him did more damage to our family than leaving him would have. It is hard to reverse this kind of trauma, and another reason I want to drive these points home. The statement, "Knowledge is power," is true. However, it's one thing to read the information and another to absorb and follow through with it.

Everyone must find the right time to escape, and you cannot blame the victim for staying. Typically, they don't know how to escape safely, and they had envisioned a happy family, not a broken, dysfunctional one. To leave would be to give up all hope of that dreamy vision, a vision the CNP paints in their mind. In my case, I didn't know what it was like to be in a broken family, so I didn't realize I had created one. It takes one sick person to ruin a family, their children, and your life. Just one. The lines "it takes two to tango" and "there are two sides to every story" are not the case when one side is mentally ill with Narcissistic, Covert Narcissistic, Sociopathic or Psychopathic disorders.

There is one story with these people: their story. They will brainwash the children against you and convince your family members that you are the reason for all the stress and dysfunction. Luckily, my parents saw evil for what it was and could not be so easily manipulated. But many families do not, siding with the calm, smooth-talking CNP.


### The One Who "Values Honesty"

This red flag is one of the easiest to spot. When you think about it, it's one of the more comical red flags. A dishonest person can be quickly identified by their statement asserting they "value honesty" or "are always honest." If a person must tell you that, it usually means they are trying to convince you of their honesty. However, someone who is honest does not need to tell everyone or make a show of being the most honest person. They are considered honest through their actions and intentions, not by telling everyone they meet that they value honesty.

This is a big red flag in both dating and business relationships because, many times, it translates to the most toxic behavior. The narcissist knows they are dishonest and therefore assumes everyone else is similar. Therefore, everything you say to them will be analyzed and doubted, for they are incredibly paranoid and aware of who they truly are. CNPs will assume you are lying when you're telling the truth. Though they know you are telling the truth, they will use this as another form of gaslighting, control, and manipulation to create drama and draw a reaction out of you. It's a constant cycle of having to prove yourself over and over until the point of exhaustion. Eventually, the perpetual narcissistic paranoia will drain you.

Another popular phrase a "narcopath" will use is "trust me" or "believe me." If you hear those words, listen closely because there is no trust to be had with them. Those words are meant solely to manipulate their victims into a false sense of security and are a dead giveaway to escape as soon as possible.


## Too Forward Too Fast

Unless you aren't looking for a long-term partner, avoid people who instantly start bringing up sex. Immediately discussing sex indicates that they don't want you for your personality but are strictly in it for one thing. Sex can be great and a part of many wonderful relationships, but in the beginning, you don't want someone to solely be interested in you based on physical features and chemistry. After all, those factors fade over time. Beauty and attraction are a small part of a healthy relationship equation. Who we are as a person tends to stay the same, especially the good parts.

Someone who wants you does not merely want what your body can offer them. They want to be in a relationship with someone they can talk to and trust. Someone they can grow with. Someone they can build a future and financial security with, not simply someone who's good in bed.

If you're going on a date hoping for a long-term, healthy relationship, you won't find one in a person who is quick to bring up sex. Those people are Narcissists or just looking for a good time, aka shallow, meaningless hookups to satisfy a primal urge versus building something substantial. They are the kind of people that rarely develop nor mature, and, like children, we'd hope they'd grow up eventually. CNPs are mentally stunted, perpetual children that want what they want when they want it, and at any cost with an inability to be reasoned with.

CNPs are very secretive; they may not outwardly ask you for sex or come on to you aggressively until they know they have you. This was another Red Flag I missed. I am an old-fashioned girl with old-fashioned values. X knew I wanted to take intimacy slow and that I was waiting until a much deeper and meaningful relationship materialized. I needed to feel loved to make love. However, I wanted to wait until I was engaged as I don't believe it's good to find out if you are intimately compatible *after* marriage.

I missed the Red Flag with this one because X was so patient, or I thought he was. I thought he was respecting my boundary. He made little remarks here and there, subtle enough that I didn't clue in until years later. I thought he was patiently waiting and felt our relationship was more than just sex. He made me believe it was, but I'd soon find out otherwise.

When we became engaged and moved into our first home together, it was time to explore our relationship more intimately. I was very adamant about X getting tested prior. He'd had many other partners, and I wanted to be safe. He agreed to testing, and it came out negative. However, closer to our wedding, I had been experiencing abdominal cramping and nausea. X took me to the OBGYN to see what it may be. She recommended bloodwork and testing for sexually transmitted diseases, which shocked me. I said that wouldn't be necessary because X was tested before we were intimate, and we were a couple of months away from marriage. Still, the doctor insisted X go for his test and said we should add it on as you never know someone for certain. At the time, I thought that was odd to say as if she didn't believe X and I were committed to each other. To my horror and dismay, our tests came back positive for Chlamydia. I was stunned and alarmed. When I questioned X how this could be, he shrugged it off and said more than likely it's a false positive, and they happen all the time.

I was young and naïve, content to believe what he was telling me rather than confront the truth. I asked the doctor, and she said while that can happen, let's be on the safe side and finish the course of antibiotics and re-test. I became terribly ill from the treatment due to the strength of the medication and a sensitive stomach but eventually recovered. X wasn't affected by the medication in the least and could work, go out and enjoy life as usual. At the same time, I was sick in bed for a couple of days due to vomiting and nausea - amongst other symptoms that I shall refrain from disclosing - from the antibiotics.

I didn't connect the dots even when it slapped me in the face! It was during my divorce when I was forced to submit all my medical files - due to him not believing I had been chronically ill for years - when I finally realized he had been cheating throughout our entire relationship.

I can recall X would not initiate sex nor make any romantic gestures. While I felt that was odd, it didn't greatly concern me, for sex hadn't been a priority of mine. Companionship, friendship, caring, honesty, and love were what I valued most. X didn't possess the same values, merely leading me to believe he did during the love bombing phase. While he didn't initiate sex, he blamed me insidiously and passively for his suffering from "blue balls." He'd explain that his rage and outbursts were due to pent-up semen, which was invariably my fault, though he made no attempts to woo or seduce me.

Only after his rages and passive remarks did I initiate intimacy to say *let me take care of you.* It felt like rape, not a consensual loving relationship. I didn't have intercourse with him from my desires nor a place of love. Rather, guilt and his manipulation drove me to satisfy his needs. He never once satisfied my own needs nor attempted to discern what those needs were together. Still, I felt shame for how much he had to abstain from sex "because of me." However, his patience for sex wasn't because he cared about how I felt but because he didn't need it from me. He was already getting it on the side with whomever. When the puzzle pieces started to come together, it was horrifying to find out all the hidden secrets and lies he kept. I had married a complete fraud, cheat, and con artist.

## Extreme Adoration

We all love to be complimented. We want to be valued and respected. However, there is a substantial difference between affection and love versus extreme adoration. Affection and love are genuine, whereas extreme adoration is a smoke screen (a ruse designed to hide one's true intentions or reality). It's hard not to get blinded by this Red Flag as it directly targets our egos. You can often spot a narcissist before getting into a solid relationship by how complementary they are to you. In the beginning, they'll complement your character or something you take pride in.

A big Red Flag is if they say, "you're not like most girls/guys." This statement generalizes both genders into a negative stereotype. When I hear that statement, I wonder what their idea of "most girls/guys" is. What do they believe most girls are like that I am not?

Other compliments include being called "my" or "mine" by someone. This may seem cute and romantic, especially since it is often portrayed as such in romance novels and movies. However, in my experience, it is something to be wary of. First off, you do not belong to anyone. You belong solely to yourself. A covert narcissistic psychopath claiming you as their own gives them power and control over you. It's different than saying she's my girlfriend or he's my husband. Specifically, statements such as "you're mine" or "she's mine" are the ones to look out for.

On my first date with X, he commented about the color of my eyes, which I didn't feel were very special as they are brown. That evening I had my blue eye color-changing contact lenses in. Oddly enough, X noticed my original eye color before we had started dating. He said, I love your big brown eyes and then proceeded to call me *his* brown-eyed girl, like the song on the radio at the dive bar he took me to after the movie. At the time, I was so flattered by what he said as we had only met once before, and for him to take notice of my eye color so early felt like he took an interest in me. Now, looking back on it, it seems a strange thing to say on the first date. He'd already claimed me after one date. Maybe if we had been dating for a while and he began calling me his brown-eyed girl after being together for some time, it would have been more normal. However, he was very forward on the first date, which is something to be cautious of and yet another Red Flag I missed. Typically, you get to know each other on the first date. Cute nicknames come later. In the case of a CNP, they want to get you hooked into them as fast as possible by appealing to the side of you that yearns to be loved.

## Mr. and Mrs. Perfect

At the beginning of my relationship with X, he responded to everything with "yes, dear." It was charming and felt very endearing and loving. Once we were married, everything suddenly became a "no," including the simplest requests like taking out the trash. I received a no when I asked him to travel less to be there for me and our children and a no when I asked him to drive our daughters to their activities when I was too sick to take them. Once he entrapped me into marriage with responsibilities such as child rearing, his perfect man demeanor completely vanished. Instead, his true love was his work, sex with other women, alcohol, and money, not his family.

This red flag is the easiest to miss. However, now that I have dealt with it, I often see it in many people, especially CNPs. It is best to be cautious around people who seem too friendly and overly agreeable. In my experience, I've trusted too quickly, leading me to be taken advantage of or hurt. People who make enchanting promises say they want to help me and talk about how they are such a good person signal red flags in my brain. Actions speak louder than words, and their actions never follow their words. If you come across a person that promises you the world on a silver platter, you may be greatly tempted to fall for their charms. All I ask of you is to keep yourself a secret from them. Don't overshare and keep it casual until you truly get a sense of the person. You can act kind and friendly with them but keep your guard up just in case. It may help to keep a "less is more" mentality.

## Very Comfortable…Too Comfortable

As we get to know other people, we tend to grow increasingly comfortable with one another. We open ourselves up to the other person, showing who we are little by little. That's how a relationship develops, by slowly opening up to another person. A CNP will do that too, but they do it carelessly. Healthy individuals remain respectful to others when they start letting them in. They should care about what you are comfortable with as well. CNPs do not care.

For example, I stayed at X's roommate's condo one night. I brought along my hair dryer, amongst other things. We had just begun dating, so what happened next was quite appalling. After X took a shower, he used my hairdryer to dry his pubic hair. Yes, you read that correctly. He knew it was mine and had no qualms about using it for his business. It didn't stop there. We had not been intimate other than kissing and cuddling, but this grown man was standing with the bathroom door open (keep in mind he shared this condo with his roommate and his roommate's girlfriend) butt-naked, blowing his crotch with my hair dryer for all to see! Why I didn't run away then, and there is beyond me. This is another reason to fully heal from a past relationship prior to stepping into another. We want our new relationship to work out so much that we put the blinders on.

When I told him how unsettling it was for him to use my hair dryer on his groin area, he acted as though I was being unreasonable and that it was perfectly normal for him to dry his private parts with *my* hairdryer. I felt confused and guilty for my disgust because of the way he made me feel in that situation. Now I understand that I was not in the wrong for expressing my feelings and that he should have respected my personal belongings. X being so comfortable using my hair dryer at the beginning of our relationship should have been a huge warning, for it showed he had no regard for my feelings or possessions. He did not ask if he could borrow the hair dryer. X used it as if it was his own. It was evident from the beginning what was mine was his, and that would become the narrative moving forward.

I was naïve at the time and did not know about CNPs. I did not know it was all to get a rise out of me. If someone shows a lack of respect for your belongings, home, friends, or family, they do not have respect for you. Respect is one of the most necessary elements in a relationship, next to love and communication. A CNP will attempt to make you feel guilt for expressing your feelings, for they believe that they are eternally in the right. It is crucial you recognize their lack of compassion and understanding before you become entrapped.

## Soulmates...or Soulhates?

Before I married X, he told me I was his soulmate. According to the stories of other victims of covert, narcissistic psychopath abuse, their exes had called them the same thing. Yet, a real soulmate would never gaslight you, drive you past the point of anger, abandon, ignore, devalue, and cheat on you, all things CNPs do. The word soulmate is commonly used by CNPs in the love-bombing relationship stage.

CNPs dole out small crumbs of praise and romantic words that keep you hanging on, hoping to fix their damaged soul.

Soulmate is another smokescreen to blind you from the truth of their actual character. How can you or anyone possibly doubt their affection towards you when they say you are their soulmate? If someone calls you their soulmate, don't allow yourself to block out their destructive tendencies. Remember that you are *their* soulmate because they can control, manipulate, and hurt you all they desire. However, the CNP is incapable of being anyone's soulmate. A soulmate should make you feel happy and loved all the time. You inspire, support, and grow with one another. You build each other up and spend time working through challenges in an adult manner. CNP's throw "breadcrumbs" at you, little amounts of good in between all the bad to keep you hoping that the façade at the beginning of the relationship will return because you experienced it and felt it.

CNPs are Soulhates. They have no soul of their own, so they must feed off others to get enough supply to keep them satiated. Once they have sucked the life out of yours, they get bored and move on to the next unsuspecting supply or, like most CNPs, already have several lined up aside from you. They do not know the true meaning of a loving relationship. Deep down, they possess hatred, contempt, and jealousy for anyone showing happiness, strength, ambition, and the desire to be more than their emotional prisoner.

## How to Keep Track of Red Flags

If I'd known this when I was younger, it would have saved our children and me from a future of abuse and anguish. I have developed a strategy that helps you identify Red Flags and keeps track of them. We often encounter a warning sign in our heads, but we either ignore it or forget it down the road. A CNP banks on you forgetting the trauma they delivered. I've learned the hard way that ignoring Red Flags will lead you straight into the danger zone.

This may seem strange or unnatural to some of you but keep a Red Flag notebook. This can be in the form of a daily journal, diary, or, more conveniently, your smartphone. If you feel something is off or not sitting right with you at any time in the relationship, write it down in your journal. This isn't for you to hold against your partner but for your security. Write down the instance and pull out this book to see if what occurred matches a Red Flag in this section or other behavior discussed.

You may format the Red Flag list however you'd like: a detailed diary entry, bullet points, writing down your feelings, or a simple red dot on a calendar. Whatever helps you keep a tally to look back on later, try it. Document everything. If you are married to a CNP, you will need this valuable history of abuse when you have finally had it, are divorcing them, or, more than likely, when they have sucked you dry enough to discard you.

Personally, I enjoy the feeling of the pen writing on paper. Although writing everything that's happened to me is triggering and challenging, getting those painful feelings out of my head and onto paper was therapeutic. I wasn't perfect, and with life and children, I rarely had time to document every Red Flag. I wish I'd spent more time documenting them all. I did write down the instances of significant abuse and could see how I justified it with false beliefs about X's real character. After all, it's hard to believe anyone could be so cruel.

Count the number of Red Flags and then determine if your partner is the safest keeper of your heart. Five to ten Red Flags warrant action, such as talking to the person about your feelings. You don't have to bring up your notebook, but rather, summarize how you've been feeling lately in the relationship. Depending on how they react, go from there. If they earnestly want to change and make the relationship healthier, they may not be a CNP. However, if they shift the blame to you, deny your feelings, and twist your words, they may be a CNP. If so, as difficult as it will be, your best option would be to run far away from them and start fresh. A CNP cannot understand your emotions nor care about your concerns. They will negatively react if something is a blow to their ego.

In the future, Red Flags will turn into trauma that is extremely difficult to heal. My book is written to help arm you against those Red Flags and stop them before they become trauma. When faced with Red Flags but unsure what action to take, consult a qualified trauma specialist, trusted friend, or family member. Often, people on the outside of a relationship see things that you cannot. Tell them about how you feel your partner has been treating you, and ask if they have noticed anything off.

Remember to be open to receiving their opinions and feelings about them. Often, as survivors, we tend to sweep it under the rug and say they had a bad day or makeup excuses as to why they are treating us poorly. If a therapist, family member, or friend has the confidence to tell you how they feel and not sugarcoat their views, acknowledge them and accept what they say as their truth. Love is blind, and sometimes you need to see things from others' points of view to get the real story. I wish I had done that with my mom as she called him like he was from the first day she met him. She had a sick sense about him, but her opinion lost value to me because she had harsh opinions about everyone. Now, had my father spoken up, I'd have listened. He tried to see the good in all and didn't see him for what he was right off the cuff like my mom.

You can produce an action plan to address these issues with your partner. Normal, healthy partners would be open to hearing your perspective, telling you their viewpoint, and working together to find a solution. A CNP would react in the exact opposite way. They will deny that anything is wrong with them, maintaining that all the problems in the relationship are because of you. They will insist that you need to change while they remain the same. No matter how much you try to change yourself, the disputes will perpetually remain the same because it is not you complicating the relationship; it is the CNP. If you get this type of reaction from your partner, you will have to accept that the relationship is not repairable because CNPs are not fixable. Don't waste your health, prosperity, and happiness on trying to help or change someone that does not want to be helped nor see any need to change.

# Chapter 2: Emotional Abuse

Emotional Abuse is one of the least talked about forms of domestic abuse. It holds little value in society, yet it is incredibly prevalent. Such abuse runs rampant in our world, the quiet killer to many young or tortured souls. Unlike physical abuse, it does not leave physical scars, at least not the type of physical scars left by another person. The scars hide beneath your skin, deep within your psyche, and are further concealed by the abuser's domineering presence. Unless you speak out about it, no one knows you're suffering, and if you tell someone, there is the terrifying chance they will shrug it off or not take you seriously. Emotional abusers have a way of isolating you from friends, family, and anyone else who may care to continue their abuse.

You may not know you're fading away until it's either too late or until you have a dreadfully long road to recovery. CNPs are exceptionally skilled at masking your emotional pain so well that you doubt whether you're hurting or being abused. The way they accomplish this is through the Cycle of Narcissistic Abuse. Once you notice the signs of the Cycle, it becomes easier to identify narcissistic abuse from the start. It is a valuable tool to have in your repertoire in case you are in the midst of a relationship with a CNP or are meeting someone new.

The Cycle is as follows:

1.    Idealize
2.    Devalue
3.    Discard
4.    Hoover

## Idealize

When you first meet a CNP or any narcissist, you will be impressed by the wondrous things they promise and say to you. Their words are their weapon. Whether they shower you with gifts and praise, tell you how amazing life will be with them, or introduce an exciting business venture that is sure to make millions, the result is the same: disappointment and damage. CNPs have a way of entrapping you in a fantasy world, making you believe that if you stay with them, everything in your life will vastly improve. They idealize based on your dreams and values. Whatever it is you share with them, they are the ones that will make it possible for you. They try to hide this from you, but the cold, hard truth is that no one can make your dreams a reality except for you. Those who make these (empty) promises to you are likely to trap you in their circle of abuse versus help you accomplish your ambitions and dreams.

A blatant sign that someone is a CNP is if they idealize or promise remarkable things. For example, in a relationship, your partner says you're their soulmate or shower you with praise (love-bombing). Or someone tells you to invest all your money into them, and they will create the business of your dreams or take you to the next level. Be wary of those with impressive aspirations for the future. Those expectations tend to crash down miserably. The idealizing narcissist is similar to those late-night tv ads we all see, the ones that tell you all about this fantastic course they teach "for free" that will tell you exactly how they became a millionaire. Then, when you watch the course, it repeats itself over and over about becoming a millionaire, without telling you how. The course may drop in a couple of helpful tips here and there to keep you from clicking off, but it never fully satisfies you. Then, in the end, they encourage you to take part in their "10-week" course for an absurd amount of money, once again promising you will learn how to become a millionaire by the end. Spoiler alert: no one ever does.

I have been taken advantage of many times by an idealizer. First, in my relationship with X, he promised me the fairytale dream life on a silver platter, saying we would retire and grow old together. That was a huge thing for me; I wanted a partner for life, just like my parents. He knew that and exploited that dream, discarding me at the exact time in life that was close to his retirement. He knew I valued family and a simple life together most of all. I faithfully stuck by him through all his insatiable work hours, travels away, lack of emotional intelligence, and abandonment of our kids and me, all on the premise of a false promise. He had sworn that while he doesn't have time for us because of work when he retires, we'd finally get that time we'd had before our marriage. He'd sworn love could get us through anything.

Love got my parents through war, famine, and poverty. Their persistence for a better life for themselves and their kids all came true. I felt it wasn't an unreachable dream because my parents had accomplished it. When X made time for me, I'd believe we had good conversations, but in reality, they were one-sided. He's a great storyteller and talker. In fact, he rarely stopped to take a breath and seemed to enjoy hearing his voice. But I was a good listener and enjoyed hearing about his achievements and projects. He never once asked me about mine. He didn't care what I was doing as long as it didn't bother what he wanted to do.

When a birthday came up, I'd ask for time with him as my gift. That was too difficult for him, and he rarely remembered, so in frustration and sadness, I asked for a check instead. I wasn't allowed to share in our accounts. He kept the one joint account depleted just enough to cause worry and fear in me about how I would provide for our children should something happen to him on his many travels. It was the worst feeling of insecurity I'd ever experienced. Why my husband would choose to hurt our children and me was a hard concept to grasp and a constant lump in my throat as I came from a family that gave real love and care. My mind was clouded, and I couldn't see the pure evil and darkness staring me straight in the face. I was in denial due to the dream I envisioned for myself and our children deep within my mind.

I was so close to my dream of growing old, with whom I was led to believe was my soulmate, only to have it ripped away by X. He never stopped lying. Just weeks prior, we had looked at a new home with extra acreage to bring our horses to. I could see he was not into it at all. He was cold, dismissive, and downright rude, yet he'd agreed to see it, leading me to believe in our future together. He argued that I was so persistent he couldn't say no. This was another lie; he was toying with my dreams. He led me to believe he shared the same retirement ideal, yet he already had plans that didn't include our children or me. If I was so persistent that he couldn't say no, how was it he had easily denied several other requests of his time throughout our years married? To throw further salt into the wound, I learned he had never intended to follow through with that promise, having been secretly unfaithful during our marriage for years.

Coverts are professional secret keepers and pathological liars. They will make up anything to keep their secrets. They have more skeletons in their closet than any cemetery has in the ground!

At the beginning of our relationship, X encouraged me to follow my dreams. A healthy partner supports the dreams of their partner. However, the difference between the CNP and the healthy partner is that they begin to discourage it later when they have their hold on you. Once we were married, X never attempted to encourage my dreams or the dreams of our children. Instead, he either snubbed them, claimed they were unrealistic or devalued anything I was interested in. I was kept so busy with all the household responsibilities, which he did not participate in, that I did not have time to grow as an individual. I lived for his needs and our children. I didn't know how to live for myself.

Instead, I was stuck in the monotony of life's chores. It made me feel like my dreams or hobbies were nothing compared to the CNPs. I felt like anything I wanted to do was worthless in his eyes. I got our children involved in trying many activities to find one they'd enjoy and be passionate about. He never encouraged that and would sabotage it by planting seeds of doubt, telling them they don't like it, or claiming it was "your mother's dream." My children did many activities that I'd never want to do. One of which was acting.

I tried one class when I was a young adult as it looked fun, and I took a drama class in high school. That was the extent of it; acting wasn't for me. My oldest daughter received one of those flyers from a popular acting school advertising, "you could be the next *Disney* star!" I knew it was a scam just to sell their courses and said as much, but my daughter begged to sign up. X specifically undermined my explanation to her that it wasn't a real agency but an entertainment group looking for more business. Rather than X and I discussing it together away from our daughter, he insisted she joins right in front of her, making me look like the villain and him the hero.

This was a common brainwashing technique he used on our children the rare times he was home. He threw money at anything that got our children to distrust me as their parent. It brings me to tears when I think of it to this day because he was slowly erasing me, and I didn't know it was happening. He was so good at it too. We aren't given instructions when you have children, but I read so many books

44

and did my best to parent with love while he did everything to put our children in harm's way. It was an extremely exhausting parenting experience. I slowly endured the erosion and division of what I thought was a strong bond with my girls. Regrettably, I had no power or fundamental knowledge of saving and stopping it.

Having children with these personality types feels like a slow death sentence and robs you of any spirit you have left. Typically, the kid's well-being and success are a parent's primary goals. However, with a CNP, no one is allowed to be better than them. They will not want their children to succeed nor be independent, prosperous, healthy adults. It's unfathomable and excruciating to think of, but you have no control. Children are very malleable and rely on their parents to protect them. The CNP will fill their brains with love bombing and the idea that they are the only one to trust, care and provide for them.

Behind your back, they erase and devalue you. There is little power to get that back once the villain parent has damaged their brains, especially the one that has the money to buy them whatever they want, whenever they want. X continues to do so to this day with both our children, including my youngest, the scapegoat. She technically got away but is still under his power as she has the desire to do things only he can afford.

Another thing CNP's do is label you as crazy to continue to devalue you, especially to your children. Years after escaping his abuse and our divorce, he continues to devalue me so that our oldest, alienated child will never reconnect. They share a common pet name for me called PB. When my youngest asked what PB stands for, I knew it had to do something with the word crazy. Typical and boring as all CNPs are. PB stands for Psycho Bitch. I went easy with my nickname for him, the "Dud." They are duds, not dads, husbands, or partners. It never ends once you have children with these covert, narcissistic psychopaths.

In the healing chapter, you will learn ways to protect yourself, but any fantasy of thinking you could save your children, especially if they are still under the control of the CNP, is unreachable. Sadly, it will be up to them to save themselves as the abuse is deep-rooted, and they have been taught you were the cause of all their trauma. This is how skillful and insidious a CNPs abuse is. The CNP's hold is strong as they've conditioned their children to have a false reality of the real world. The children won't want to see the actual truth because the toxic parent's world has been the fun world, and they are trauma bonded to accept the crumbs thrown at them.

What child doesn't want to be loved by both their parents? They hope that the toxic parent will change, and they will feel loved. They will cling to that hope. Saying anything negative about it or trying to open their eyes to how they've been manipulated will further cement you as the bad parent in their mind. It's futile; instead, focus on yourself and setting *boundaries*, which I will discuss in further chapters.

Lastly, X promised me we would build a family together. Emphasis on together. X ended up never being there, either on countless business trips or affairs. I raised my children chronically ill and alone, save for the assistance of mother's helpers I had to hire to take them to school or their hobbies, as he was rarely there to do so. Most of the time, it felt like a family of three, my two daughters and I, rather than the family of four he promised it to be.

However, I didn't solely experience the idealizing CNP in relationships but also in business. One of the hardest parts of my divorce was selling my dream home. At such an emotional time, I hired a real estate agent to help me find a home and sell my current one. I still didn't know much about narcissism back then, so when the agent promised to find me my new dream home and sell my current home quickly, I believed her. After all, she was a professional with a code of ethics. What could go wrong?

For starters, she encouraged me to send a low-ball offer on homes I was very interested in. Unfortunately, I lost the homes to better offers. Also, she wasn't providing me with any homes to see. I had to do my own searches because I was being forced out by X and the private judge he hired during our divorce. When I found another home I was not entirely satisfied with, she promised everything would be perfect.

In each home we went into, she illustrated a false narrative on the condition and features, which I found quite annoying. I wasn't completely sold on the home we decided on, but I was also desperate. My concerns included a hill above it, a lack of privacy in the backyard, and the possibility of mold. She painted the picture that this home could have fruit and privacy trees planted, and a beautiful white fence could be put up on the hill as there was nothing to protect my small dogs from the wildlife.

I asked for her to provide the rules of the HOA to make sure, but she did not. I found out she was wrong after I purchased the home under pressure from the court and financial duress. It turned out that the homeowner's association did not allow what she had claimed could be done. Still, I wasn't willing to fault her just yet. People make mistakes, of course.

However, it got worse. When I opened the kitchen drawers, I noticed black spotting. I said it looked like mold, and the realtor immediately disagreed, stating it was common usage staining and that the owners kept their home impeccable and well-loved. She told me there would be no mold in the home, discouraging a mold check. I am allergic to mold, and when it came time to check that mold box on the contract, I hesitated. My doctor suggested that I check the house for mold before purchasing. But, given the pressure of the divorce, private judge, and X, I had no other home choices in the area due to a lack of inventory and upcoming winter holidays and thus made the purchase hopeful there would not be any mold.

When it was time to pull up the severely urine-stained carpeting, an intense odor wafted through the home. I received a phone call from the contractor informing me we should get a remediation company to test the home for mold immediately. The odor was intense. Indeed, there was mold in the home. Had I not known about it, my health would have been significantly compromised, something the agent knew, for I had vehemently expressed how allergic I was to mold.

The final straw occurred when she broke her promise to sell the family home quickly. Not only did she move out of state during the sale of my old home, but she turned buyers away due to her vacations and house hunting in the other state she was moving to. She triangulated X by lying to him, saying I was the cause of the home not selling. She lied to potential clients, claiming I was not allowing people to see the home. This, in turn, was used against me in my divorce case, as getting the home sold was a requirement. She further interfered with my case by calling the lawyers on my dime, leading me to incur exorbitant fees on a contract already near expiration just to hold onto a sale she could not accomplish. I was appalled. How could someone be so unprofessional?

The realtor gleefully trash-talked my ex to me, saying she was on my side while texting him behind my back about things I never agreed to. The situation added more stress and financial damage to what was already a devastating time. She became so deceitful that I had to hire a private investigator to expose lies so I could fire her and find a new agent. X didn't want to find a new realtor as he enjoyed his ability to further abuse and cause distress and financial abuse to me.

Miraculously, I succeeded in doing so, and our home sold within a matter of weeks after I posted the new agent's ad on all my social media. Had I not initially fallen for her idealizing act, I could have avoided financial burden, stress, and anxiety. My knowledge of covert narcissistic abuse was in the early learning stages as I devoured any article and book I could find and read. It takes time to learn all the tricks and deception these people use.

Idealizers are everywhere, including teachers, engineers, employers, doctors, lawyers, psychologists, sports coaches, etc. One of my daughter's coaches was infamous for her false promises and lies. She would go on about all the competitions she won in the past and that she would take you to those competitions but never followed through. There was some excuse about why they couldn't go to a competition, but none of those excuses ever included the truth.

We'd found out later that she was banned from those competitions, which she never wanted us to know. As time went on, her idealizing promises became increasingly absurd. She would talk about new facilities people she knew would build for her that had all these desirable features. Yet, those plans never came to fruition. She ended up getting kicked out of facilities rather than creating any.

Furthermore, she expected her young students to keep secrets from their parents, wanting them to trust her instead. Expensive items purchased would often disappear, and when confronted, she'd gaslight, release her crocodile tears, and blame shift onto the children for being careless with putting away their items. We knew our things were being lifted by her sticky fingers. Only when I'd call her out on her hogwash would our belongings mysteriously reappear. Still, many items were never recovered.

Time and money were wasted on what "could be" or what "would happen." Had we left earlier, my daughter would have been happier, more confident, and more advanced for her age and length of time spent in her sport. Still, my daughter and her friends were attached and possibly trauma bonded to this CNP coach. It wasn't until all her friends left did my daughter get the strength to follow. I had no choice but to leave this decision to her as she was adamant for me not to be involved and was a young adult at the time. When she finally saw the truth, she left. Since then, she has been much happier and significantly improved. When you remove yourself from a toxic individual presence, you will be amazed at how much better your life can be.

Do you now see the danger of the CNP idealizer? Not only do they raise our hopes, but they waste valuable time and money in the process. If you can recognize someone idealizing and avoid them, you will be all the better for it.

## Devalue

As I mentioned above, my ex often devalued the hobbies or dreams I felt the most passionate about. As a result, I would feel unimportant and self-conscious about the things that used to make me happy. I can remember X's words to me very clearly.

"You choose things that are beyond your ability."

Those were discouraging words, especially from my partner, who should have been uplifting. People dream, and those who dream and follow through can achieve anything they wish. However, it's much more difficult when you have someone telling you to set your expectations lower daily. When a CNP devalues you, you feel inconsequential, like an object, because that is how they see people. You must remember that the psychology of these individuals has nothing to do with you. You happened to be the unfortunate recipient of their destruction.

With a CNP, their devaluing flies so low under the radar that it is virtually unnoticeable. It's deeply felt yet not easily placeable. You find yourself unable to explain why you feel so insignificant and small. Devaluing occurs as a backhanded compliment, passive-aggressive remark, or slight judgment passed.

I didn't realize it at the time, but the devaluation started early in my relationship with X. Our first actual date was a joint outing with my brother and mutual friends at the movie theater. We arrived much earlier than the rest of our party, and I wanted to wait until the rest of the group arrived. X didn't want to and insisted it wouldn't be a problem if we got our tickets immediately. Not wanting to be difficult, I agreed. However, when everyone else arrived, the movie we had already bought tickets for ended up selling out.

At this point, I was quite nervous as he was nine years older than me, and we didn't know each other very well. A close family friend of mine had introduced me to him, and I trusted that friend's judgment of character. X had recently broken up with his girlfriend, or at least that is what he told me when he asked me out on this first date. Feeling a bit isolated from the rest of our party, I still went forward with the date, ready to enjoy the comedy movie we had gotten tickets for.

Throughout the movie, everyone in the theater, including me, was laughing. However, X did not. When I asked why he didn't laugh, X said the movie was dumb and not funny. X carried himself with an air of intelligence. Hearing him say this about a movie he saw me enjoy made me feel beneath him in intelligence. I admired intelligence and accepted his opinion as fact simply because I did not feel my opinion had a higher value than his own. That is the power of the narcissistic devalue. They hold themselves with such higher regard than anyone else that you feel what they believe has more value than what you believe.

Throughout our relationship, X consistently made disparaging remarks about things I wanted to do or what I was passionate about. If I talked about a dog breed I loved, he would reply with some news story he heard where the dog had attacked a human. If I expressed my passions or something exciting in my day, he barely paid attention, falling asleep in front of my very eyes while I spoke. I felt insignificant to him. When someone makes it seem like what you have to say isn't worth their time, that is devaluation.

Another example of devaluation can be procrastination on tasks the CNP considers beneath them but are important to you. Whenever X wanted to do an activity of his choice, he would be punctual and make time in his busy schedule to do it. However, when I asked him if he could take our children to their after-school hobbies, he would arrive late to pick them up from school or drop them off late at the activities if he agreed to do it at all. Most of the time, X would say he was too busy to do it or had a meeting and more important matters to take care of. Yet, he seldomly seemed to have a meeting when it was something he wanted to do.

Passive aggression can be the slightest remark or lack of action that creates a negative stigma surrounding something you like or need. The remark does not sound outwardly mean to ordinary passersby or anyone listening. It simply seems like a regular comment. However, when directed towards you, it leaves you feeling devalued. You don't concretely know that it is happening, but you feel it emotionally. Words never reflect the actions the CNP makes. Passive aggression is dangerous this way. Someone can demean, insult, and hurt you as much as they like without looking like a bully or the bad guy. Passive aggression can invariably boost the CNP's image to other people while simultaneously tarnishing your own.

Another form of passive-aggressive behavior X would demonstrate was that he would become the hero in everyone else's eyes except his wife and children. If the children or I were being bullied or mistreated, he'd fully support the bully versus us. One example was from our children's polo club. They had an overtly narcissistic polo coach that taught more drama than polo instruction. She didn't like our oldest child because she wasn't as fast as the others. She had some learning disabilities, which many of her teachers were frustrated by. Rather than the coach working through a plan to bring success to our daughter, she verbally attacked me and my parenting.

Instead of supporting me, X decided he would be the coach's savior, empathizing with her and telling her he would solve the issue by removing me from the equation. I was happy to exit that toxic situation and knew it wouldn't last but a day or two before she'd be fed up with him. He didn't pay the bills on time, was consistently unavailable and out of town, non-responsive with communication, and did nothing to teach our daughter what she needed to do to appease this unhappy coach.

Within two days of him taking over, the girls came to the club to find all their polo gear thrown in garbage bags for them to pick up and embarrassingly drag to their car in front of all their friends. None of their friends were allowed to speak or look at them, or they would be kicked out of the polo club.

Where was X? On one of his many cheating trips with his secret affair, enjoying his life. At that point, when he finally heard that his plan didn't work out, he raged and spewed forth profanities at the coach. I witnessed two narcissistically injured narcissists yelling over each other, and it wasn't a pretty sight. They were two grown adults, yet both had toddler minds. It is simply not feasible to reason with those who make it their goal to be as unreasonable as possible.

As part of human nature, we often fear judgment. If one is devaluing through the passage of judgment, this targets that innate fear within us. When someone judges you for something you enjoy, it immediately makes us feel like we are doing something wrong. It is important to remember that if you enjoy something, that is what matters the most. Anyone else's opinion should never trump your enjoyment of what you do. If someone tries to devalue something you love, take a step back and acknowledge how you felt at that moment. Did you feel upset, judged, uncomfortable, or self-conscious? If so, realize it is not the thing you enjoy creating those negative emotions, but rather the person or people who devalue you. You must stand up for the things that make you who you are, and if anyone tries to tear you down, they are not worth your time. Instead, focus more on doing what you love rather than pleasing others.

# Discard

X and I were together for 27 years, twenty-four married, and all abused and used. Soon after the wedding, the love bombing stopped, and an immediate shift in personality began. I can't remember one loving or special moment we shared, no matter how hard I tried. He was glued to his work and his computer. Other than the birth of our children, which came with many challenges and abuse, I have no fond memories with X. Chronically ill, homebound, financially, physically, and psychologically abused, I was at the lowest point of my mental and physical health. I didn't believe in divorce nor want to put our kids through it. I chose to put up with him, clinging to the hope that things would get better. After years, he knew his kept secrets were so unforgivable and despicable that he cowardly sent an email saying, "*maybe* we should move on."

The email provided no clarity, reasoning, or explanation. Instead, it was aloof, unfeeling, and a cruel, cowardly way of ending a twenty-seven-year relationship and marriage. I felt blindsided, the world ripped out from under my feet. I'd had a set future, a home, and financial security for my children. Yet, from one singular email, X took it away. Since being chronically ill, I cannot freely leave the house, trapped within the confines of my physical limitations. Still, I did right by my children, raising them solely on my own in the best way I knew how, while he was never around. None of this mattered to X when he discarded me, moved out, and left me with little to nothing.

Anything I got from the divorce, I had to painstakingly fight for, all for it to end up in the lawyers' pockets. In an unforgiving justice system that often favors the abuser, I was at a loss many times. X held many secrets, words spoken from his mouth were lies, he withheld funds and account information, and pretty much any discovery from our financial wealth during our marriage. He cried poor any chance he got and would tell our children; that mom ruined his retirement funds. X wanted and kept all our money. He intended to leave me in ruins and debt. Covert Narcissistic Psychopaths want to destroy you and are good at doing so. It's their ultimate game, which they won't stop until they have succeeded in your demise.

In the discard phase, the CNP essentially dumps or discards you. Unlike a typical breakup, there is no closure at the end of the relationship. You are left with little to no fond memories as if they never existed. For, in truth, it didn't exist. The CNP moves on quickly while you are left reeling for quite some time. The truths you find out during the discard phase are appalling. You discover lies and secrets you would never have thought possible of the person you loved. They act unexpectedly as their mask slowly begins to crumble. Everything feels like a fraud or as if you've been tricked. Nothing about your relationship will feel natural. The CNP throws their victims out like trash as if they never existed nor mattered. It does not feel human or moral but rather torrential and soulless.

You will wonder why and how the CNP could leave you easily, quickly, and with little explanation. Most of the time, when people break up, they've tried everything to solve the problems in their relationship first. They go to therapy, talk about it, and implement changes. A healthy breakup includes both sides of the story, with both parties understanding why the relationship didn't work. No matter how horrible breakups can be, you are still left with a sense of why it ended and that you tried your best to make it work. You can take what you learned from that failed relationship and apply it to another. This is significantly more difficult with a CNP discard as they discard without explanation.

If they participate in therapy, it is done to triangulate the therapist against you. They paint you as the unstable one and themselves as the victim. A CNP makes therapy about themselves, but not in any effort to change their behavior. When the therapist tries to give you homework for both of you, it will only be done by you. The CNP does not want to change and does not feel they have any problems to work on other than their issues with you. All fault lies with you because you didn't want to be enslaved by your abuser.

I tried over nine different marriage therapists with X. Each one gave up and urged me to seek a divorce. They all said they couldn't help me, and he would never change. He would never accept my disability, and either I put up with him or get out. I could sense they all thought I should leave him, but at the time, I didn't understand the severity and wanted to keep trying.

Several therapists recommended books that didn't click in my mind back then: *Trust After Trauma: A Guide to Relationships for Survivors and Those Who Love Them* by Aphrodite Matsakis, Ph.D. and *The Body Remembers: The Psychophysiology of Trauma and Trauma*

*Treatment* by Babette Rothschild. I purchased and started to read the books but felt they didn't pertain to me at the time. Now I realize how trauma bonded, and in denial I was. I had severe Cognitive Dissonance from years of gaslighting, blame-shifting, projection, silent treatment, and psychological and physical abuse.

Cognitive Dissonance is a severe state of doubting the reality of what is occurring in one's relationship. Covert Narcissistic Psychopaths are exceedingly secretive to the point that you realize you don't know who the person you married or were in a relationship with is. The CNP will take no blame for the relationship ending. They will insist that you were the ruin of the relationship and that *you* were the abuser.

Then, they will move on with their lives as if you were never a part of it. They find a new human supply, get a fancy new home or car, go out with friends, and carry on as if they didn't just end your entire world. The CNP will be utterly fine while you are left in shambles. And the worst part is, that's what they want. They want you to be left emotionally ruined because it gives them immense pleasure.

Though they discard you, don't be fooled into thinking that is the last you will see of the CNP. The CNP never wants their supply to end, and they will do whatever it takes to keep it going unless they know their old supply has figured out just how nefarious they genuinely are.

## Hoover

We've reached the end of the cycle, the part that starts the entire process over again. This is the part of the cycle in which the CNP tries to lure their victim back in. CNPs don't like to give their supply up for too long. They want to keep you stuck in that cycle of narcissistic abuse, forever feeling empowered by your misery.

Hoovering allows the abuse to continue, occurring once the CNP discovers your desire to escape and move away. It is a form of emotional blackmail in which they either use guilt to reel you back in or contact you out of the blue as if nothing has ever happened. They will start the love bombing tactics all over again, saying they can't live without you or they dreamt about you. It's all manipulation to bait, con, and lure you back into their endless cycle of narcissistic abuse.

The CNP will try to convince you they've changed, that they are back to the person you fell in love with. Different hoovering techniques they use include ghosting and then contacting you when you least expect it, being overly apologetic, showering you with gifts, threatening to harm themselves if you don't come back to them, promising you the world/future faking (painting a heavenly picture of a future with them), and going as far as spreading more lies about you to instigate a response. You, unwittingly, become their supply once more. However, as soon as they have you back in their clutches, they return to the narcissistic abuser they were before.

Hoovering doesn't just occur after a relationship has ended. It can happen during one as well. When X and I got into fights, he would come back later with gifts, buying things to get back in my good graces. When my parents visited, he would act like the perfect husband. I often thought of it as two weeks of good and then months of abysmal treatment. Such behavior allows the abuse to continue. The CNP comes back with a love bomb, but as soon as you believe they've changed and are back to the person you fell in love with, the narcissist reappears.

Throughout the cycle, the CNP will employ multiple different tactics of emotional abuse to keep their victim constantly on edge. To avoid these tactics and protect your mental health, the best chance you can give yourself is to remain educated on all the forms of abuse they utilize. If you aren't sure whether your partner is a narcissist or CNP, note which of these tactics they use. The more methods they practice, the more likely they are a toxic individual.

Recognize the pattern of abuse and manipulation, set solid and clear boundaries and stick to them, prioritize what you need, and try not to absorb or internalize their hurtful comments. Most of all, Grey Rock, if you are stuck until you can completely ignore and avoid engaging with them. The only way out of their insidious game is to leave and stay No Contact.

## Push/Pull – Lack of Object Constancy

Push/Pull behavior occurs when the CNP treats you well, then switches up and treats you poorly. Their reward-and-punish tactic invokes a trauma bond between the abuser and the abused. This trauma bond keeps you trapped in their push and pull cycle. They use humor, kindness, and generosity to charm you, only to sabotage it for no apparent reason. Once you begin to feel the loss and pain, they switch back to their love bombing game. It's all temporary and will never last longer than a couple of weeks. Some can carry it on a little longer, but, in my case, the kindness and generosity lasted all of two weeks. The twisted mind games of push and pull are all to manipulate and control your psyche.

CNPs are cruel because they *lack* object constancy, which is the ability to still have an emotional bond with someone when you feel angry, disappointed, or hurt by them. You know it is temporary, but you still have feelings and an emotional connection for them at their worst or when they aren't physically around you. Individuals with covert narcissistic, sociopathic, or psychopathic traits project these negative feelings towards another as their ultimate focus and fixate on it until their disordered need for your suffering is cultivated. Just as they don't genuinely love you at your best, they never love nor empathize with you at your worst.

CNPs are remarkably deficient in human compassion, have no emotional IQ, and lack sincere attachment. They don't have guilt and remorse nor take accountability for their poor and abusive behavior. The other person will be at fault in their skewed eyes. CNPs cannot handle the idea that the person they are in a relationship with doesn't fit into their perfect partner and how they believe they should act and behave. They move on to their next target or victim when they realize they are with an actual human being with emotions and faults. Hence, the lack of object constancy. The connection between you and the CNP means nothing to them other than as a means to an end. Their incessant need for praise and attention is limitless. They can't self-soothe and rely on others to keep their ego inflated. CNPs refuse to be alone and will demand you sit with them through all chores or tasks they do not wish to do. You are nothing more than a punching bag to a CNP.

## Flying Monkeys

A narcissist and CNP keep a harem of "flying monkeys." Flying Monkeys are people the CNP keeps close to defend them, hurt their victims, and communicate to others on their behalf. They are typically family members and close friends of the victim who fervently participate in the CNP's smear campaign of you. Anyone with the potential to hurt the CNP's target is fair game for the CNP. The more people you're close to, the more the CNP wants to get them on their side, so when you start seeing past the CNP's mask, you end up alone in the effort. Flying monkeys help the CNP keep you feeling isolated and self-doubting. They are exceptional at gaslighting and denying reality. They spread out the smear campaign started by the CNP and generally enjoy creating drama. While some flying monkeys may be under intense manipulation and brainwashing by the CNP, others are cut from the same cloth.

Still, it is more trouble than it's worth to convince a flying monkey to see the truth about their favorite CNP. To protect your mental health, the best thing you can do is to separate yourself from the CNP and their flying monkeys. Regardless of whether they are your closest friends or family members, and you believe they can change, it is best to still separate from them so that they can see the truth for themselves. This will be one of the most difficult boundaries to set for yourself, especially with family members. Remember that friends who support the CNP were never your friends, to begin with.

However, in my case, my adult daughter became one of X's strongest allies and flying monkeys. To accept that your own daughter could be so hateful and joyous in your suffering is an entirely new level of cruelty. Still, I had to disengage, Grey Rock, and, finally, go No Contact with her. The flying monkeys will be treated very well when the CNP targets you. They won't see nor believe any abuse is occurring. Therefore, to save them, you must leave them behind to see reality. She wasn't in her right mind and became merely an extension of her CNP "unfather." I will never call him a dad or father. Child rearing and love award you the title of father, not just the procreation process. X will never be a real father, for he is entirely incapable.

X was the biggest delegator; if it meant he didn't have to do something, he was content with putting others out and paying for it, especially any dirty work he wanted done. He never wanted to get blood on his own hands, so he had others do it for him. When selling our family home during the divorce, the real estate agent became a flying monkey with X to create more financial drain and hardship during the selling process. She'd add me to group chats with him, which I asked her to please never do, and complain about how I prevented clients from viewing the home. As I discussed earlier, she did everything in her power to continue X's smear campaign against me, including sabotaging our house sale to the point I needed to hire a private investigator.

More flying monkeys during the divorce included his sister and the girlfriend he had for years behind my back. Both searched for a home for him during our divorce as he didn't put much effort into finding the home himself. His sister went as far as trying to sell our youngest daughter's horse behind her back. She was clearly a flying monkey and had no regard for her niece, her sole prerogative being to do her brother's bidding.

When X emptied all our accounts and investments – a court violation - a lot was put into gold and silver bars and coins which his sister drove across the country to pick up and drive back in an RV to hide it further so that it would not be split equally. Absolute madness. He used our oldest daughter, his girlfriend, and his sister to drain our girls' college fund, leaving nothing for our youngest as she was his scapegoat. He knew he could manipulate our oldest into dropping out of school as he never encouraged her to stick with any activity or schoolwork that became challenging.

X cried poor to everyone when, in reality, he made over a million a year just in his paycheck. He had multi-million-dollar investments, all of which he stole, including any money I earned in the marriage that I trustingly put in our joint account. He siphoned the money in our joint account, leaving nothing in it for our children and me to survive on. It was extreme financial abuse vehemently inflicted upon me for wanting to escape his endless torment.

Hold on to your reality to fend off the CNP's flying monkeys. When the CNP or their flying monkeys try to make you doubt yourself, remain secure with your thoughts and beliefs. Remember that you are worth believing and that the majority isn't correct. Connect with new people who aren't gaslighters, those who let you speak your thoughts and don't invalidate them. Disengage from the flying monkeys as best you can.

Lastly, seek therapy. It can be excruciating to say goodbye to cherished family and friendships ruined by a CNP. Having someone to talk to about your feelings in a healthy manner is profoundly beneficial to your healing and future happiness and fervently urged and necessary.


## Passive Aggression

Passive Aggression is a significant way CNPs emotionally abuse their victims. They never appear like the bad guy to anyone watching and to you. Yet their words still strike true. The words they use and untold meanings shift into your thoughts until you believe them yourself. You wonder what you're doing wrong to hurt the CNP or why you feel like a failure. The CNP won't outright tell you what they think you're doing wrong nor confront you directly. Instead, they use different techniques to make you look bad while maintaining their perfect image on the outside.

X was the king of passive aggression. It was a chronic daily occurrence while we were married and during our divorce. His passive aggression was very subtle and unnoticeable by outsiders and our children. While the kids were present, it was directed toward me to make me look like the bad parent.

X knew how important a healthy lifestyle was to me due to my medical background. I wanted to raise our children with an understanding of what foods were the most beneficial to their bodies and overall health. I didn't want our children to suffer as I did, and I had been raised on a junk food diet. X sabotaged my efforts every time he took the children out, buying their love with various candies or desserts instead of a sustainable lunch or dinner. X taught our children instant gratification was more important than mindfulness of healthy habits and caring for their bodies.

"Don't tell your mom," X warned them, implying that I would punish them if I found out.

It was an unnecessary warning. Laughably, my youngest child often came home with chocolate surrounding her mouth. When I asked her about it, she readily spilled the "cocoa" beans. I was not mad, nor did I reprimand them, but I was hurt that X could care less about their health or what was important to me.

X telling the children to hide things from me was a passive-aggressive way to instill a lack of trust in their mom. Whenever he was out with the girls, he would make subtle comments to insinuate that I was the "bad cop" and not a safe, caring mom. Not only was this passive aggression, but it was also devaluation.

Another form of passive aggression in CNPs is procrastination. While we all procrastinate occasionally, we don't typically do it to upset the other person. However, for CNPs, procrastination is one of their primary tools to irritate and wind up their partner. It's considered passive aggression because the person doesn't tell you "no" or that they don't want to do it. Instead, they tell you they will do it but put it off to the point where you either end up doing it for them or it becomes too late. If I implored X to take the garbage out, do the dishes, or remove his dishes from where he left them out, he'd procrastinate, saying he would do it later and ultimately "forget" to do it. I was picking up after him. At home, he was a slob, but at another person's place, he would be the first to clear up his plates and everyone else's. I'd yearned for him to extend that same courtesy in our home, but he never did.

Another example of passive aggression occurred during dinner time. If the girls and I were enjoying our family dinner, which he rarely participated in as it interfered with his meetings, he'd complain that I didn't call him to join us. Not only did I text him, call him and send a girl in to get him, he'd ignore us or shoo us away, saying he was busy and would be another 5 minutes. An hour later, he'd show up moody and blame me for not including him. The rare times he did sit down with us for dinner, he wanted us to remain quiet and attentively listen to him go on and on about his work which the girls didn't understand, and I'd heard over and over like a broken record. If we didn't, he'd act like a victim. When we dared to laugh or joke together, he'd say we were joking at his expense and not including him. All this behavior was to get attention solely on him. His passive-aggressive remarks made us feel bad for not including him, though that wasn't our intention. Rather than join the conversation normally, X commanded our attention through the manipulative techniques of passively guilting. It is difficult to be angry with someone at the moment for trying to keep the attention on themselves when you don't realize that is their objective. Instead, the CNP makes you feel ashamed for excluding them, something most people don't wish to do to someone they love.

Passive aggression is done to confuse the victim and make them feel guilty while making the CNP look innocent to any bystanders.


## Projection/Blame-shifting

One of the most harmful types of emotional abuse is Projection or Blame-shifting. A practiced CNP can effectively compel someone to feel guilty for or take the blame for something they didn't do. According to their logic, anything the CNP does wrong is either your fault or something you did. This kind of abuse leaves the victims with severe guilt. Since CNPs typically target the most empathetic people, guilt is the fundamental emotion they play on. They know empaths place themselves in others' shoes, so they consequentially exploit that. CNPs will bring up their tragic past or recall something you did that you may not remember. They will say whatever it takes for you to forget the awful thing they did and instead admit guilt to something you didn't purposefully do.

The term blame-shift or projection can be used interchangeably. To explain how both terms relate synonymously, let's consider an example. Most classrooms in school have a projector. What does a projector do? It projects images onto an empty wall or whiteboard. Of course, the wall and the whiteboard alone don't contain those images. Instead, the projection device displays the images onto the empty area. Intrinsically, CNPs are projectors. The very thing they blame you for is something they did. Rather than owning up to their malicious intent, they project that corrupt image onto you. Suddenly, you aren't an unblemished, blank wall. Instead, you're covered head-to-toe in whatever wretched act the CNP performed. To the eyes of the CNP and their flying monkeys, you are at fault because all they see is you.

Most of the time, when a person walks into a classroom, they see the whiteboard first. The projector is a small device attached to the ceiling or, if it's an older device, behind the teacher's desk, an object of little significance until its subsequent use. The CNP wants you to be the whiteboard people see first, so it is easier for others to accept that you are at fault. We may not like to see the images a projector exhibits, but we do not fault the projector for showing those images. The CNP wants people to look upon you in horror while they remain unnoticed, free of condemnation.

With so many people doubting you, it's hard not to question yourself and wonder whether the CNP is right. Under the condescending and confrontational glare of the CNP, people often find themselves admitting to something they didn't do, only to realize too late that it simply wasn't true.

My ex was phenomenal at blame-shifting. To avoid a tremendous amount of stress when X took our daughters to their activities, I had to create a highly detailed schedule with the names of people they were meeting, the times the girls had to be at places, and any other vital information that couldn't be forgotten during the day. I got the girls ready, packed their lunches, and prepared the schedule every day so everything would go smoothly. However, no matter how much preparation I put into the day, I would still get blamed for some small thing that went wrong. X would call me angrily and tell me I missed something on the schedule. He blew it way out of proportion, causing stress for the children, creating a scene, and starting a fight with me. Also, though he was the one that wanted the schedule for the day, he would consistently call me a micromanager to our daughters, insisting that I wanted to control everything.

He wanted lunch/dinner to be made, so he didn't spend money on food. I made enough food for the entire day, but he took the children out to eat anyway, and their food containers returned full. Still, he blamed me for having to spend money on eating out. Later, during the divorce, he wanted me to reimburse him for all the meals he chose to take the girls out for.

A darker example and one many feel uncomfortable about is how CNPs use projection to manipulate their victims sexually. As I mentioned earlier, my ex would say that because he didn't get sex from me every time he needed it, I was the cause of his blue balls. Therefore, it was okay for him to throw things around the house, slam cupboards and doors, be destructive, and create fear because his sexual needs were not met. That is abnormal behavior. Sexual abuse in relationships is especially an issue for women who are told they aren't meeting their man's sexual needs. However, what needs to be discussed is how women weren't put on this earth to meet someone else's needs sexually. Women deserve to feel emotional safety and to value for who we are as human beings, not for the needs we can fulfill. People are not objects and should not be treated as such.

A sexual relationship is built on trust and love, not fear and threats. No person should ever push another into having sex when the other does not feel up to it or comfortable. While sex in a healthy relationship can be wonderful and contribute to the relationship, in a toxic relationship, sex can be dangerous. CNPs use sex to further traumatize and isolate their victim. They claim that if you don't want to have sex with them, there is something wrong with you, not them. This couldn't be further from the truth. If you don't feel comfortable with having sex, especially because someone is pushing you into it, then that is a reflection on the other person. Remember: you don't owe anyone sex. It is something that should be enjoyed mutually.

I will never forget the day my ex became physically abusive to me. I'll go more in-depth into the story in Chapter 5, but that day I learned how dangerous a CNP can become and how their blame-shifting can twist into something truly terrifying. Although X physically assaulted me in front of my daughter, he never apologized to me for what

72

happened. Instead, he insinuated, as all CNPs do, that I was the one to blame. It is the ultimate manipulation when an individual successfully blames you for an act of physical harm they committed. That is how many survivors of domestic abuse get trapped in their toxic relationships for so long. By not taking the blame for their actions, the CNP can continue abusing as long as their victim believes they deserved the abuse or it was accidental.

However, physical and mental abuse are never deserved or accidental. Abuse that repeats itself over and over will never stop until you realize it is not *you* who is at fault but the *abuser*. Once you lift the blame from your shoulders that the CNP has tried to weigh you down with, you can finally run free.

## Pathological Lying

CNPs are cowards, so they rarely ever tell the truth. The one in a million times they are truthful are usually smokescreens to keep you from realizing their dishonesty. The cowardice of their mind and soul leads them to keep enormous secrets and lie throughout life. Typically, when you first meet a narcissist, especially a CNP, they'll butter themselves up with all their accomplishments, how knowledgeable they are about a particular topic, or how talented they are at something, to name a few.

My ex spun a tale to anyone he met that he was an experienced high-level black belt in Tai Kwan Do, an innovator in his career, and a terrific father. He was none of those things. He paid an exorbitant amount of money to gain upper degrees on his black belt without competing, training, or working out. He paid for the ability to boast to anyone who would listen of his great prowess in martial arts.

As for his career, he boasted about how he practically created the internet and was a leader in his company. However, after talking to those who've worked with him, I learned that he often took other people's work or ideas as his own and profited from them. He also was not as high up in his company as he made himself seem.

X loved telling people how great a father he was when he somehow found the time to take his daughters to their events or activities. He'd claim he was the best because no other father did that. X put himself in photos with the kids, and if I didn't post it on social media, he'd guilt me profusely until I did so. X would ensure the photos of him and our children were good while the ones he took of our kids weren't the best.

I would have to beg him to take photos of our girls. He made sure to fill the files up full of all the other children there with a sprinkling of our own. He'd promise photos for all the other parents, which led to hours of work for me to edit and separate them all so that each parent had their own folder of photos. I'd be up all night working on the photos for others and realize the ones he took of our kids didn't show them in their best light.

If I dared offer him constructive criticism, he'd lament over how inconsiderate I was of his time and efforts, that he was doing this for me, and that I should be more appreciative. Towards the end of the marriage, I hired a photographer and would receive the most beautiful photos I cherish to this day. It was cathartic to delete the horrendous, guilt-laden photographs he took.

X spun so many lies and exaggerations to boost his image that it was difficult to believe anything he said. His greatest fabrication was his commitment to our marriage, relationship, and children. X led a secret life, traveling lavishly, fine dining, drinking, and sleeping with others while blaming me for spending too much money on our children and necessities. He had no remorse, no inclination for responsibility. X wanted to live the good life and lied with ease to everyone, unwavering when confronted with solid facts. Pathological, compulsive liars have no care for anyone and use lies to manipulate. They get away with such lies, for they believe it as their truth. It's gaslighting on steroids.

## Gaslighting

Gaslighting is the most common way a CNP abuses their victims and occurs when someone attempts to make you feel as though you are going crazy through manipulation. The ultimate goal of gaslighting is to drive someone to question their sanity. The term originated from the 1944 film, *Gaslight*, in which the antagonist turns the gaslights on and off while at the same time denying that he saw any change so that his victim would think she had gone mad and was seeing things. Nowadays, Gaslighting is done more psychologically. The CNP will do something morally wrong or treat their partner terribly and then deny it ever happened.

They will convince others in the victim's social circle that they are wholly innocent, so no one else believes the victim. This makes the victim feel isolated and question whether the CNP is the problem in the relationship. Gaslighting exists in relationships, business deals, the workplace, and products or services. The premise of gaslighting is to turn the attention away from the wrongdoer and instead make it seem as though the victim either made it all up or is simply confused.

Before studying Narcissistic Personality Disorder, I had never heard of the term gaslight. Now that I've learned what it is, I can identify when someone is attempting to gaslight me or others. Gaslighting isn't solely something a narcissist does. In fact, many people do it to cover their mistakes, forsake accountability, or use it in self-defense. However, when a CNP gaslights, they intend to confuse, disorient, and isolate their victim.

Some gaslighters will purposefully misplace your items or destroy them and say they have no clue how it happened or where the item is. Gaslighting was a sport for X. He would purposefully misplace his items and then get upset at me if I didn't help him find them. It became a daily stressor as most items were right in front of his face. When I pointed it out, he would say it wasn't there before, and then I would have to immediately stop what I was doing and show him exactly where it was.

X would misplace his car keys, saying he would be late to our children's doctor's appointments, school, events, or activities the rare times he was around to help take them. Oddly enough, anything that was of value to him, usually something he needed, his work or his hobbies, was never missing. If asked to do a house chore such as washing the dishes, X would say he couldn't find his gloves. Therefore, X couldn't do the dishes as he didn't want his hands to look like mine. My hands, dried, inflamed, and cracking from constantly washing the dishes and being allergic to the gloves, wouldn't have looked so bad if X could have pitched in and shared the chores.

The most traumatic form of gaslighting he used with me was his schedule. Anything needed for the kids or me had to fit his schedule, which was wholly packed. If something wasn't scheduled into his calendar, it didn't exist. If I told him about it, he would end up "forgetting." Maintaining the schedule was time-consuming as he wanted everything added, including when the kids had school, their holidays, play dates, activities, etc. When I needed his help taking the kids somewhere, I had to schedule it, tell him about it, and then remind him about it.

I did everything he asked each time, and then he would say I never told him, he didn't see it on the joint calendar, or I didn't send him a reminder. I would feel frustrated to the point of crying because not only did I schedule it, but I sent countless email and text reminders and verbally reminded him as well. I couldn't have been more diligent in maintaining this schedule, and when I needed help, it was because I was too sick to do it myself. The frustration of him saying I hadn't done it or that he hadn't seen it on the schedule was overpowering, overwhelming, and done with the intent of causing incredible stress and confusion.

We lived by his schedule, and when the girl's activities were booked in empty time slots, he would say it never appeared on his schedule and therefore didn't exist. I would show him on the computer where I put the activities on his schedule, and he would continue to say it didn't come in on his end. Therefore, he didn't get it and had no time due to meetings. Then, I had to scramble last minute to find outside help, finally just hiring a mother's helper because he was unreliable.

The most liberating feeling was petitioning for divorce and deleting that calendar forever!


## Guilt-tripping

One of the most painful types of abuse a CNP will inflict upon their victims is the Guilt-Trip. This is especially damaging to Empaths or empathic people. CNPs love to make people feel guilty, especially when convincing someone to do their bidding or when they are being called out.

Throughout my life, I've dealt with guilt trips from my mother and my partner. If something bad happened to me, my mom would say, "God's punishing you." I would believe it, creating a very unhealthy mindset that a higher power was looking down on me with an iron fist, ready to punish me for anything I did wrong.

Then, with my ex, anything he couldn't or wouldn't do ended up my fault. X knew I suffered from severe Endometriosis, but he was never empathic about my pain nor acknowledged my health challenges. However, some of his worst guilt-tripping involved sex. He wouldn't initiate sex in the way most couples do. There were no romantic gestures, moments of affection, foreplay, or anything to bring about a close connection. I'd thought that was strange but had dated one person prior to him, so I didn't consider the oddity of it all as much as I should have.

However, he guilted me through sporadic rages out of nowhere, claiming his anger was caused by abstaining from intercourse. He'd hurdle into fits of anger, yelling, throwing items to scare me, punching doors and walls, and swearing profusely. I was intimidated into giving him pleasure. He'd take over if I couldn't satisfy him, beating himself off feverishly like a wild animal in heat. It wasn't attractive, let alone intimate. Yet, I still had to remain unclothed and near him, with one of his hands on my breasts until he finished.

It felt like rape, not lovemaking. In those moments, I felt more like an object that he needed to release his sexual urges with. Still, I had the guilt of not being a satisfying enough partner. He made me feel as though I was depriving him of sex by not enjoying it. How can one possibly enjoy it when their partner never tries to make it pleasurable, comfortable, or loving?

For an empath, guilt-tripping sticks for a while, making you want to change and be better for the other person. By continuously trying to improve yourself and be what the other person wants you to be so that you don't have to feel guilty for upsetting them, you end up losing yourself in the process. That's one of the ways a CNP strips their victims of their identity. Then, when the CNP discards the victim, who has lived years of their life for the CNP, the victim is left wondering where to go from there. CNPs make everything your fault while never taking accountability for their own actions. It is you who must apologize, never the CNP.

When you have done nothing wrong, the other person implies whatever unpleasant situation is somehow your fault. They make their unhappiness evident so that you go above and beyond to help.

Different ways people try to guilt-trip include:

1. Point out how much they've done for you or how much hard work they've done to make it seem as though you aren't doing as much.
2. Make passive-aggressive remarks about an issue to show they're unhappy without explicitly stating why.
3. Refuse to talk about the problem or use silent treatment.
4. Deny that they're upset but show you they are through their actions or body language.
5. Point out specific things they did for you, such as, "Remember when I did ___ for you?"

This leaves the person feeling that nothing they ever do is good enough. Guilt-tripping in a narcissistic relationship is done with the intent to manipulate. Once you notice it reoccurring often, along with other abusive behaviors, you must develop a safe plan to leave the relationship. The way to fix a toxic relationship is to end it and go No Contact with the person.


## Financial Abuse

Financial abuse is another favorite of CNPs, especially wealthy ones. If you depend on a CNP for money, they will use it against you. To the CNP, any money you spend, be it for you or your shared children, is an extravagance, a burden, and a drain on them. Financial abuse connects to guilt-tripping as the CNP often makes their victims feel guilty about whatever they purchase. If you aren't the one spending the money and the CNP bought you a gift, they will still use it against you. In their next guilt trip, they'll list all the things they bought you and spent money on that you "never use" or aren't showing enough appreciation for. You don't love or appreciate them enough though they give you the world.

However, the CNP will never give you what's important: love, compassion, and respect. They may shower you with superficial presents, but emotionally, they won't be available. Furthermore, gifts are given at a cost and as a means to take away from you. Nothing is offered out of the goodness of their heart. It's as if they do not possess a heart, for they are quite mechanical in their thinking and void of feelings.

As a survivor of narcissistic abuse, I know firsthand how it feels to be financially abused. Chronically ill and homebound, I did my best to find work-from-home jobs, raise our kids and be the best mother I could be. With X gone all the time, the responsibility of taking care of our children was left solely to me. While X went on business trips, in which he would spend extravagantly on hotels, restaurants, dates with his secret supplies (affairs,) and more, I stayed home to care for our daughters, manage the house, and hire help to take the girls to their activities.

X would complain about how much money we spent on a mother's helper, but he was rarely there to help take the children anywhere as needed. If we had no helper, our daughters wouldn't be able to go out and enjoy activities with their friends or play sports. My illness kept me homebound as going out was traumatic due to nausea, IBS, suffering, pain, tiredness, and tetany. With the unpredictability of my stomach, driving is as much a risk to me as it would be to someone drunk or too tired. It is a danger I didn't want to put my children in. Not only that, but my immune system is deficient, and when I catch something, it affects me more than it affects others.

Therefore, having a career and earning enough money to provide the lifestyle and education I wanted for our children was not an easy possibility. This was before the pandemic era, which has made working remotely more accessible. Still, I put all the money I earned into our joint account and everything into being a good mother and a faithful wife. It was never enough for him. Although we had the money to provide a good education and life for our children, he complained, saying he didn't want to spend money on it as it jeopardized his retirement. He didn't want to buy safe vehicles for our children to give them the freedom to get to school without needing help. Any money that went towards the betterment of our children was considered too much. However, money spent on traveling, restaurants, hotels, car rentals, his affairs, etc., was perfectly acceptable to him.

He created the idea that we had no money to spend and that spending his money was wrong (unless he spent it). I found out about the secret millions he hid and hoarded in the middle of our divorce. He was much more well-off than I ever knew and ever expected. Still, he cried poor to our children when they asked him to support their college education, telling them he was living "pay-check to pay-check." He would guilt-trip them about any money he had to spend to support them by telling them how little he had left because "your mother took it all."

In reality, I received very little from the settlement and certainly nothing to live off of. X claimed he made a piddly amount of money from his job, less than the national average, though he is in one of the highest positions in his company, making a bountiful salary. Yet, somehow, a now single mother with a chronic illness and no job had more money than him.

Financial abuse is serious and often overlooked by the legal system. In fact, during a divorce, the legal system opens the gateway for more financial exploitation, with most domestic violence cases involving financial abuse. Several forms of financial abuse exist, such as preventing the victim from working and earning their income, controlling all the financial accounts without allowing visual access to them, and subsequently, using money as a mechanism for entrapment.

X was extremely controlling over our accounts, creating numerous spreadsheets that detailed every penny spent within our family, conveniently excluding the money he spent. He was abnormally territorial over his mail, vulnerable to fitful bursts of anger when the mail wasn't immediately directed to his office. The envelopes contained dozens of different financial institutions that I had neither any knowledge of nor participation in. When I asked about them, irritation clouded in X's eyes, and he scornfully dismissed my question, claiming they were investment accounts he managed.

Anytime I requested the passwords to our financial portfolio so I could budget appropriately, he was too busy and promised to show me later. A promise he would never keep. I lived in worried ignorance of our finances, pondering what my children's and my future would look like should tragedy take his life. I never felt financially safe or secure.

I was permitted one credit card for all the household and children's expenses. Though I bought for necessity, each month, X would throw the statement on the table, berating me for spending beyond our means. Later, after having to subpoena financial discovery materials for the divorce, it became apparent that I could have never spent beyond our means. Frankly, the X was the one overspending. It is devastating to have endured years of anxiety over finances only to learn none of that stress was necessary.

X frequently wouldn't pay the bills on time, incurring penalties, poor credit (under my name), and leaving medical bills to go to collections. Since he oversaw paying the bills, I had no knowledge of whether they were paid or not until I became notified of his inconsistency. Not wanting him to incur additional late fees, I began paying overdue medical bills, adding to the charges on the credit card statement. Still, X criticized every financial decision of mine, insisting I learn to budget. Although, I had no freedom to know what our budget was. He decided the major financial decisions and constantly drained the joint account, siphoning money into dozens of private accounts under his name. His double standard when it came to spending was confusing and frustrating. The skies were the limit when it came to him and his relatives, but spending for myself and our children was heavily weighted.

I felt like a child having to ask for money from my parents, though I had never felt that way with my parents. X would approach me in the middle of the night to force me to sign financial and tax documents with no explanations and without allowing me the time to read them thoroughly. He knew that I would be too exhausted to argue.

X never paid into our family home, mortgaging it as much as possible, so there was little equity in the property. Although he could easily afford the house, X forced me to sell some of my investment stock that I had acquired outside the marriage to put for the down payment. We could have outright bought the home with our community funds, no mortgage needed, which was a great shock to learn later as I deeply loved that place. Losing the home was painful, knowing we had the funds to keep it. When it sold, I received nothing from the sale as X dragged out our divorce to cripple me financially. Instead, the money from the home sale went directly to the legal teams.

Financial abuse is draining. The feeling of inadequacy eats away your soul like a slow-moving but deadly parasite. Financial abuse becomes substantially more potent throughout a divorce and will be discussed in more detail during the Divorce chapter.

Being a stay-at-home mom is no easy task but is often overlooked. Many do not realize that you aren't earning credit for yourself as a stay-at-home mom, making it difficult to get a mortgage or loan, pay legal bills in the event of separation, and provide for your and your children's basic needs. CNPs use financial abuse to entrap you, relying on your inability to afford to escape. They want you to feel as though you can't survive on your own without them. At that point, the relationship becomes strictly transactional, and the CNP will gleefully guilt you for your financial reliance on them. They will create great distress over any money you spend, pick and choose how you spend it, and eventually leave you with nothing.

Anytime you ask them for money, the CNP will act as though they are doing you a considerable favor, one that you should deeply appreciate. Voicing concern over how they treat you calls for immediate financial punishment as they threaten to cut you off. You should never have to ask anyone if you can purchase something. That choice is your own. However, you must be financially independent to make those decisions for yourself. It is difficult and often frightening to step out on your own and rely on yourself for money, but well worth it in the end.

What I wish for you to take from my story is the realization that you are not the cause of the CNP's financial distress. In fact, they may not be struggling with money at all! The best way to escape financial abuse is to find a way to support yourself. Have a backup plan, even with a healthy partner. Relying on anyone for money stirs up resentment and allows the other person to hold it against you. Keep your boundaries strong and, if they insist on breaking them, realize how toxic that individual is before it's too late.

To avoid financial abuse at the start of the relationship, be wary of people who claim they want to take care of you or spoil you. That can be nice initially, but as you grow older and the other person gets more comfortable, they may use it as an abuse tactic later on. Financial Abuse is a form of coercive control that is very degrading, controlling, and restrictive of your freedom and ability to escape from your abuser.


## Triangulation

Narcissists frequently practice Triangulation as they relish pulling in a third person to use as their ally against you. They use it as a manipulation tactic to maintain control over situations. The person the triangulation is directed towards often feels ganged up on, left out, and ignored. The victim of this attack may begin to doubt and question themselves, wondering who is truly in the wrong. The idea is to bring another person who isn't directly involved in the conflict to take the CNP's side. This leads you to question whether your feelings are valid because an outsider is also against you.

In relationships, CNPs use Triangulation to maintain control. They rarely use blatant abuse tactics, making their red flags so subtle. Keep in mind that people can unintentionally triangulate, usually when they feel they need support to defend themselves. However, CNPs use triangulation to hurt, which you need to look out for.

For example, let's say you and one of your roommates are arguing over who cleaned the bathroom last. Your roommate might bring in the other roommate to confirm that they cleaned the bathroom and that you hadn't done it in a week. This is not narcissistic abuse but rather addressing conflict.

Now, let's say you don't feel comfortable doing something the CNP asks you to do, so the CNP tells your sister the situation from their point of view and asks your sister to support them and tell you to do it. Now, you have two people pressuring you to do something that doesn't feel right to you. You'll feel ganged up on or as though you did something wrong. The CNP is especially successful when they triangulate you with someone close to you or someone you deeply admire. You'll be more influenced to listen to what the CNP says if another person you hold affection for agrees with them.

It's essential to understand the distinction between regular triangulation and abusive triangulation. Consider whether it makes you feel devalued and ganged up on. Evaluate whether the request is simple or unreasonable. If you feel more pressure and discomfort in the situation, chances are, you've come across the red flag of Triangulation. Note that situation in a journal, on your phone, or anywhere you can keep a record of it for yourself. If the triangulation occurs too often, then don't ignore it. Break free before the abuse has a chance to fester and grow.

X's go-to victims for triangulation were our daughters to create fights between us. For example, during our divorce and on my birthday (CNPs love to disrupt and ruin birthdays and holidays), X told my youngest daughter she needed to pick up her stuff from his house as he wanted more garage space. If she didn't come immediately, he would donate it all. Panicking about her belongings, my daughter told me about it and wanted to go pick up the stuff.

However, our new home was much smaller and already full of the rest of her belongings. We had agreed she would split her things between the two houses, taking her most essential and cherished items for our home together. Given that it was my birthday and we had already agreed on what to keep at each place, I held my boundary and advised her to ignore X's immediate concern for another time. It is important to note she only had a couple of boxes at her father's place, which he could've easily kept without losing any room in his large garage. However, the stress of X's demand and my unwillingness to give in to his ridiculous request on my birthday, which he knew I would disagree with, led to an argument between my daughter and me. He had set it up so my daughter would panic, get anxious, and take his side, making it look as though I was unreasonable for not letting her bring her stuff home.

Once we both recognized what he was doing, we made up, and my daughter told him he could go ahead and donate it all if that was what he wanted. Ultimately, he didn't donate any of it, knowing she wouldn't visit him if he did.

Another time he triangulated me with my daughters was during our first family discussion about the divorce. He and my oldest daughter ganged up on me, saying it was my fault that the divorce was happening. He led my oldest daughter to believe she was the one who convinced him to end the relationship because of how I treated him in our marriage with little to no regard for the way he treated them and me. To involve your daughter in such a private and sensitive decision without ever discussing it with your wife is beyond cowardly and twisted.

They took it to another level when my oldest suggested I hook up with his girlfriend's ex-husband as he didn't enjoy sex. I had never discussed sex with my daughter, so I couldn't fathom how she discerned my preferences. What was X telling her, and how could she suggest something so preposterous? Clearly, X involved her much more than she ever should have been. X never took responsibility for any of his cruel and disgusting behaviors. This was not only triangulation of our daughter but emotional incest, which I will further expand upon in the coming chapters.

## Pathological Compulsive Lies and Cheating

While this one is the most apparent abuse, it's still ignored one too many times by the CNP's ability to manipulate and get their empathic partner to forgive them. If you find that your partner lies continuously, especially about integral details, save yourself the trouble and don't give them that fourth, fifth, or sixth chance. If your partner cheats on you and comes back to you saying they still love you and it was a mistake, they will do it again. You will be happier with someone who wants to be faithful to you rather than hurt you.

Cheating is never the other person's fault. If the other person is unhappy in the relationship, they should communicate that to you rather than cheat. Problems can be solved with honest communication. Cheating expresses a lack of communication necessary for a strong relationship. Forgive them once, and they'll learn they can do it again, casting the blame on you instead.

My ex lied to me about his secret affairs. It went a step further as he was with another woman for over ten years while we were married. At the beginning of our relationship, I told him to let me know if he or I ever felt the desire to cheat or if he found someone else. I wouldn't be mad or destructive, but it would allow me to move on. However, X never gave me that chance. Any time I suggested that he was unfaithful, he blew up, guilt-tripped me for having the idea, and ultimately denied it. X still denies how long he'd been having the affair. After I found out about his cheating, he still claimed to want to try to make our relationship work. This was just another tactic to keep me as his narcissistic supply. However, I knew there was no longer any trust whatsoever in our relationship. At that point, it was time to move on.

It is not your burden to "fix" or reform a cheater or a liar. You are not responsible for the problems that led to those behaviors. There's a difference between supporting someone in what they're going through and making excuses for their behavior. In situations of deceit and cheating, put yourself first. After all, the other person didn't consider putting you first before acting, and in the end, you will be the one getting the most hurt. Cheaters are cowards; they don't have the respect or decency to communicate their unhappiness. And they have no desire to fix things, only to continue damaging. When someone has revealed themselves to be untrustworthy, take that as a sign to keep your guard up and stay true to what is evidently in front of you, rather than the story the pathological liar attempts to spin.

## Smear Campaign

The Smear Campaign occurs at the beginning of relationships, the middle, and the end of them. When you're on a date with someone, and they start talking about how toxic their ex was, that red flag is waving like a flag in a windstorm. If that person is comfortable talking badly about a past relationship to you, someone they first met or are just getting to know, they will undoubtedly do the same about you. This is apparent in friendships as well. I used to feel special being the one my friend confided to me about another person they didn't like, only to feel surprised later when they hung out with that friend acting very chummy. I would think, *didn't you just talk about how much that person bothered you?* Later, I realized my friend would smear me similarly to other people.

In relationships, you don't know the ex that is the target of a person's smear campaign, yet you are expected to judge someone you haven't met. Isn't it strange to mention things their ex did that they didn't like? This is because they are already trying to condition you to be the partner they want you to be. However, you will never live up to the standards of the CNP because they are not wholly satisfied beings. No amount of changing yourself or trying to be better than the ex they talked about will make them appreciate you more. When you finally realize it and move on, your ex will start talking about how toxic you were to their next victim.

On my first date with X, he immediately began trashing his ex, saying their relationship broke off because she was emotionally unstable and unprepared for anything serious. I believed him at the time, but now that I know about these tactics, I realize that he was projecting himself onto his ex. He was emotionally unstable and couldn't put the necessary work into a relationship. Not only did he smear campaign his ex, but he also continued to see her from time to time. He would tell me about those visits, expecting a reaction from me, but I never felt jealous and merely shrugged it off.

The smear campaign can be used to abuse the CNP's victim further after the relationship ends. One of the cruelest tactics they use the smear campaign for is to turn your children against you. They constantly devalue and smear you to your kids. This is so that they brainwash them to hate and not trust you. It works against you but, unfortunately, the children too as they can't feel real love and parenting. They are taught that parenting is abuse and that you are using them for personal gain. Isn't that ironic? It's more projection because that is precisely how they see their kids.

Their kids are an extension of their arms to serve them. They are a tool in the narcissist's toolbox. Smearing the loving parent builds a lack of trust within the child, alienating them from you all the easier. They use parental alienation in divorce as their ultimate weapon. After all, the greatest hurt they can inflict on you is the loss of your living children. The CNP takes immense joy in spreading false information about their ex to all their flying monkeys and people in the victim's life. They can give you a bad name at your workplace, within your friend group, in your local neighborhood, etc. It's another way for the CNP to stay on top while everyone else is squashed beneath them.

The best way to deal with a smear campaign is not to give anyone any reason to believe it. Do your best to rise above the CNP's hate by appearing unaffected, unbothered, and, if anything, a little amused. When their flying monkeys try to get a reaction out of you by telling you what the CNP said, act bemused rather than offended. Say, "How interesting" or "Did they?" and then shrug it off as if it doesn't matter to you. That will confuse the instigators who expect you to react explosively as the CNP told them you would. CNPs will smear campaign their targets, but you can take power back by rising above their cruel words and making them look like fools.

## Silent Treatment

The silent treatment is a destructive abuse tactic in which the CNP or unhealthy partner refuses to communicate verbally with or acknowledge the other person's presence. Discomfort, stress, and frustration are all desired emotions the CNP hopes to instill in their target. It results in the victim worrying about their own behavior rather than that of the CNP, leading the victim to take responsibility for something they didn't do so the abuser will speak to them again.

My first real relationship was much better than my marriage but still unfortunately toxic. For the sake of this story, we'll call him J. Any time a guy looked at me, despire the fact the person was a total stranger, J would become filled with jealousy and give me the silent treatment for days. He would disappear, breaking contact with me completely. The only communication he made with me was horrible letters using many *colorful* words saying I was a terrible person and accusing me of cheating on him. He wholeheartedly believed I had something going on with any guy who looked in my direction or smiled at me. He refused to talk to me or acknowledge my presence when his jealousy was triggered. I became exhausted with his abrupt change in demeanor and eventually broke up with him.

Using the silent treatment in relationships makes the target of the silent treatment feel unimportant and minor compared to the other person. It creates an unequal balance of power in the relationship dynamic. It significantly damages parent-child relationships as the parent makes the child feel like they don't matter. Children who have grown up with silent treatment often feel desperate for affection and validation, leading to more toxic relationships later in life.

I received the silent treatment as punishment from my mother many times as a child, and both men I had serious relationships with ended up being just as destructive. The silent treatment makes people unsure of themselves, modifying their personality and behavior not to upset anyone again. Victims constantly fear rejection and isolation from the person they love.

The way to deal with silent treatment effectively is to take a step away. In some circumstances, that may mean leaving the relationship entirely. However, when you don't have much choice, try to enjoy the silence instead. See it as a break from conflict and take that time to focus on yourself. It is essential to know that a person is giving you the silent treatment because they lack the empathy and maturity to deal with conflict healthily. You are not unworthy because another person can't handle their feelings.

Instead, set healthy boundaries and distance yourself. Pull yourself away from the relationship as best you can, either by keeping it casual or putting less stake in it. A person who utilizes the silent treatment, especially a covert, narcissistic psychopath, will never change. Therefore, you must protect yourself from their torrential abuse by using their silent treatment as an escape. Don't plead with them to speak with you or promise that you will change. They are the ones who need to change. If you concede to the silent treatment, their manipulation has succeeded, and they will do it again. Instead, walk away and enjoy some time to reflect.

When my youngest daughter asks her father for something she needs, especially via text, he often leaves her hanging by either not replying at all or responding to another text instead. This causes her to feel guilty for asking or worried that she upset him as he did not deign to decline verbally. Rather than giving her a straightforward answer, he leaves her with the hope that he will eventually reply and the anxiety that he is upset about her asking for something. This silent treatment control tactic makes asking him for what she needs to feel unsafe and uncomfortable with the effect of her not doing so again. Rather than simply giving her an answer, X covertly manipulates the conversation and her emotions with the silent treatment.

I guide her through those situations by encouraging her to pursue the question further and not just letting him "forget" about it. Whenever she needs something, we construct the question in a way that expresses how helping her out would benefit him as well. CNPs will do nothing out of the goodness of their heart. Anything they give or do must, in some way, benefit the CNP. However, you can utilize that fact to your advantage. The next time you need something from a CNP, instead of having to go through the fingernail-pulling torture of their mind games, formulate your request in a way so that it leads to the ultimate advantage of the CNP. Whether it be improving their reputation, boosting their ego, etc., pinpoint what the CNP values and use that to your advantage to gain a temporary win over them. Bear in mind that a CNP catches on to tactics quickly, so make sure to get what you need and go No Contact as your final resort.

## Intimidation

Intimidation is a scare tactic to exert control over the CNP's target. They may become aggressive, yell, throw or break things, punch walls, etc. By intimidating their partner, the CNP asserts that they are capable of physical harm, leaving their partner in a constant fight or flight mode. Intimidation builds up. You may think that the CNP won't punch a wall again or raise their voice anymore. However, their words provide a false sense of comfort, for the intimidation and love-bombing to follow are all intentional on the CNP's part.

Not all narcissists utilize physical abuse. CNP's prefer mental to physical, as it remains unseen by outsiders and is just as potent a poison. As discussed earlier in this chapter, under Guilt-tripping, X would explode violently to get what he wanted. In his case, it was sex. He was also performing intimidation. I felt afraid during his violent outbursts, and because of that fear, I gave him what he wanted. He intimidated me to give him something I either wasn't in the mood for or simply didn't want to do because of how he made me feel.

The most malignant narcissists and CNPs will intimidate their victims into submission. If you find yourself intimidated by someone,

98

it is important to take a few deep breaths and stand your ground. Otherwise, they will continue to do it again to you, knowing that it worked. However, if you feel you are in an unsafe situation, try to remove yourself as best you can, either by calling a friend, family member, or the police if necessary. Giving them what they want out of fear never fixes the problem. Instead, it creates a greater issue that can spiral into something far more dangerous.

One of the most dangerous times was when X was drinking. He is a closet alcoholic who drank by himself daily in his office and excessively drank when out with friends. That's when most of his rage came out to play. He'd have little patience and look me straight in the eyes with soulless pits of seething hatred that I can't begin to describe. If I stood up for myself during these moments of rage, he'd throw things, punch walls, slam doors, break dishes by slamming them in the sink and dish rack, throw books or nearby objects, and, at worst, push me until I fell to the floor or into a furniture piece close in proximity. X wanted to control me by carving fear into my heart.

If you see the CNP in a fit of rage, walk away, find a safe place that you can stay, and escape. In this stage, all they see is red and hatred.

## Word Salad

Word Salad is typically associated with mental illnesses such as schizophrenia, denoting a type of speech that is nonsensical and confusing. However, concerning narcissistic abuse, word salad is used to bewilder the CNP's target. Word Salad is a gaslighting technique in which the CNP tosses out words that don't make sense in a solid attempt to divert one's attention from the issue at hand or make their victims doubt themselves. The term can also describe how CNPs contradict themselves, making you second guess what's true and what isn't. If you start experiencing word salad, there is nothing else you can do other than a step away from the conversation.

An example of word salad I received was from a narcissist who had claimed he could help fix my disability vehicle. He was a con artist who damaged my vehicle more and refused to refund me, when he had previously agreed. For background information, my daughter took my vehicle to this repair guy to fix it, and he had left, claiming he would be back in twenty minutes, needing to get a part. Instead, he left for over an hour, got lunch, and was virtually unreachable. He had told my daughter it was too dangerous to drive the vehicle, only to contradict himself later and tell me it was perfectly safe to drive it. After so much waiting, I told my daughter to come home. This was his exact reply to the matter:

*"Be there and he didn't understand what was taken off nothing to be worried or unsafe I had the parts but the one glued on the tank wasn't adjustable and drilling through your coach isn't an option so yes if I had known she was waiting for our return I said it would be 20 to thirty getting the parts pieced together it's made up of 6 different sizes and try finding in a mess at the plumbing dept at Lowes any way u win I'm 4 hours over due flat rate gets the win. I'm now losing money other jobs passed up on to accommodate your needs and I*

*promise your budget was not going to change. $183.00 is all you owe*
*the $3800 I paid was an un for seeing size difference in the mounting*
*of the gate so it will be easy to pull. Etc"*

All of this was said in one text and made no sense to me. The only things that stood out were the con artist's blatant attempts to blame-shift the situation onto me, saying "I win" for getting a flat rate rather than paying hourly for a service that could have ruined my vehicle. Note the added exorbitant amount of money "$3800." The service my vehicle needed did not cost anywhere near that price, but his adding it in was meant to confuse me and have me wonder what he meant by that. Was he saying I owed him $3800 for a part? Was he talking about his financial duress? He mentioned it as a distraction because he ghosted us for an hour and didn't finish the job. Rather than simply explaining why he was gone so long or the misunderstanding, I received a large text filled with word salad.

That's when I knew it was futile to entertain him any longer. Though I wanted repairs on my vehicle as soon as possible, I resolved to wait longer for more reliable service than to go through the whirlwind of stress from a narcissist.

You will notice that when trying to have a different opinion than the CNP, you will be thrust into an endless loop of verbal diarrhea, blame-shifting, and a nonsensical spew of words meant to distract from the main issue. With my CNP ex, most of our arguments stemmed from him not participating in our marriage. If I asked for something, he would go into a long explanation about how he doesn't have time due to work or taking a nap. Then, he would start pointing out completely off-topic things, such as me not bringing food to him in his office or calling him for dinner (although I did; he just ignored it). He would continue with endless hot air to the point that I would blow up, just wanting him to be quiet. It became chaos and confusion. During one pointless argument, I plugged my ears and walked away like a child.

At that moment, I felt disgraceful and realized I was losing control of the person I am due to all his nonsensical chatter and chaos. Sadly, before I realized what he was doing, I let him get the better of me in front of our children, which furthered his smear campaign that I was unstable and not one to trust.

We all wish we had known, but one can never grasp the true depth of these diseased minds. CNPs are masters of deception and are aware of exactly how they're treating you. They prey on your innocence, trust, and desire to try to make things work, problem solve and find a resolution. A resolution that will never happen with them or their endless arguments and word salad. It's another tactic to drive you mad.

By the end of our marriage, I stopped blowing up. Instead, I left the room, unable to deal with X's endless excuses and confusing arguments. At that moment, tranquility began to return to my nervous system. Still, there was more work to do. I had to escape to heal.

## Lack of Empathy/Emotionally Unavailable

The central characteristic of any CNP is their lack of empathy. In the beginning, you may think the CNP is the sweetest, most caring person. However, the actual value of a person's empathy is not in what they say but more in what they *do*. CNPs will butter you up with how they want to take care of you, how much they love you and claim you are their soulmate. If you pay close attention, you will see there are no actions put forth to support these empty words spewed from their rotting mouths. Did you notice your CNP's breath? It was rancid and rotting. No mint could cover that up. They are spoiled from the inside out, and their smell never dissipates; it only worsens as they age.

When it comes the time that you need their emotional support and love, they won't be available. They'll be partying with friends while you're sick with the flu. If your close relative passes away, they'll complain about how you're not giving them the attention they deserve. This red flag is very indicative of a CNP and difficult to spot. You must be diligent in recognizing the timing of their actions and how they behaved in moments of vulnerability instead of believing the CNP's version of the story. After all, the CNP can spout lengthy speeches about the empathetic person they claim to be, but without the proof to back it up, all they have are empty words.

In the middle of an argument, you could pour your heart out to the CNP, and they will show little empathy or reaction. Their faces are blank slates, void of emotion and virtually unreadable. They may simply walk away, dismissing you entirely. Such nonchalance makes their victims feel unheard and unloved. Later, they'll return and try to get in your good graces again without resolving the earlier conflict. It constantly feeds into the same abusive cycle.

X's lack of empathy was chilling at times. I would cry, yell, or spill my soul to him, and he would stare back at me, face void of emotion, except for a subtle smirk playing across his lips. The narcissistic smirk. Many survivors of narcissistic abuse have a shared experience with the smirk. When you're in pain and desperation, the narcissist shows their pleasure with a chilling smirk. It is one of the only indications that they are using you for supply. The timing of their smirk is inappropriate, showing off their arrogance and condescension. The smirk stays in your mind as you wonder what could have made them smile in such a profound moment. Visually, it is indistinguishable from a typical smirk, but once you've seen it in a dark moment, you won't forget it. The smirk shows the CNP's lack of empathy, but once again, it is so subtle that victims usually explain it away in their heads.

Furthermore, it is a smirk of disrespect, contempt, and pleasure in your suffering. Once you take time away from the narcissist and remember your arguments, the smirk will come back to haunt your thoughts. Yet, once you identify the narcissistic smirk, it becomes another green light on your path to escaping the abuse. Going No Contact with a CNP is your next step toward freedom.

## Isolation

CNPs isolate you from the outside, from your family members, and yourself. They don't want you to rely on anyone but themselves for attention, affection, or love. Your world must revolve solely around them. By isolating you, it makes it harder for you to escape their control because you will have no support to run to. They can continue abusing you over and over as long as they have you isolated from the people that care about you.

Red flags of this behavior typically include subtle digs or negative statements about your friends or family members. It won't seem very impactful at the time, but the words stick in the back of your head so that you question the friend's or relative's intentions the next time you see them. They enjoy making random, slight comments about people, so you feel compelled to ask them why they feel that way. Then, they'll make a big deal about not wanting to tell you to ensure you keep pressing them on the issue. Once the CNP is satisfied they have you gripped to their every word, they'll smear campaign the person until you feel the same way they do about that friend or relative.

They may also smear campaign the victim to the victim's family and friends. They will get on the good side of people you're close with and manipulate them against you. Again, this is all very subtle. Be on the lookout for how close your partner is with your friends and family. You may want them to have a good relationship with the people you love, which is healthy, but ultimately, you need your friends and family to support you more than the person you are dating.

When I spoke about devaluation, I mentioned an example from one of my first dates with X. During the date, X separated me from the rest of the group we were supposed to be going out with multiple times. By isolating me, he was able to use his manipulation tactics without interference from the outside. There was no one to support me or back me up if I needed it. He also isolated me from his friends, making me feel left out each time.

It is uncomfortable to be isolated and ends up making you more dependent on the CNP, which is what they ultimately desire. He went as far as to isolate me from his family, my family, and our children. He wouldn't involve me in any of his trips with our kids, and when I tried to phone, he said they were too busy and would talk to me later. Later would come and go; still, I received no word from him or our children. I didn't feel like part of the family but, instead, an outsider trying to look in. He tried hard to smear me to my parents, but my mother saw through his evil ways and would turn it around on him.

This led him to have great disdain for my mom, and he smeared a very loving and giving grandmother to our children. Our oldest child believed him, for he successfully alienated her from my mom and me during the divorce. My mother was quite happy to be rid of him, but losing one of her granddaughters broke her heart. She never fully recovered from that loss and was hopeful we'd all come together again before she passed. Sadly, that day never came for her, and I don't suspect it will for myself either. Some children believe their lies readily because they need that parent to love them. Yet, they will never receive that affection and instead lose out on love from other family members that care for them. Many children of narcissistic abuse become just like the narcissist and repeat these patterns of abuse to the next generation.

There comes a time you must let go, regardless of your relation to the child or family member, as brainwashing is hard to break, and they are too filled with hatred and the belief in the CNP's lies. The damage is done. Sometimes you can do reunification therapy, but that depends on the child. Many alienated children will do whatever it takes to protect their narcissistic parent, and your efforts lead to nothing other than more pain. It's an unfortunate loss for all.

## Violates Boundaries

Boundaries are critical in a relationship. Without boundaries, hurt and resentment proliferate, poisoning the relationship instead. However, once you set the boundaries, you must ensure the other person respects them. That isn't to say you should create too strict or unreasonable boundaries. Set healthy boundaries for yourself and your partner and encourage them to do the same.

Violations of boundaries to look out for as possible hints for a toxic person and CNP include your partner mocking your boundaries, disrespecting them, making you feel guilty about creating boundaries, and flat out ignoring them, creating negative boundaries in retaliation.

One very traumatic event that occurred before having kids with X was the time I couldn't attend a *Cirque De Solei* show with him as I was too sick and suffering from a UTI on top of it. He never accepted nor acknowledged my health issues and still wanted to go. I didn't want to be the cause of him not going, so I encouraged him to see it. We were staying at my parents' home while they were away on a trip. I had brought my two older dogs with me as they had grown up in that home. However, I made sure to watch them while they relieved themselves outside, as my parents had a pool in their backyard with no fencing around it.

When X returned home, he demanded my full attention so he could talk about the show. I asked him if he could wait until the dogs finished doing their business. Rather than respecting my request, he grew upset with me and guilted me into sitting down at the table while he ate. I didn't want to leave the dogs, but I felt threatened and too drained for another fight. I sat down, leaving the sliding door open so the dogs could come back inside on their own. My younger dog returned relatively quickly, but my older guy didn't. I had a terrible, sinking feeling that he had fallen in the pool. When I ran outside and found him lifeless under the pool cover, I cried and screamed in utter agony at the top of my lungs. I quickly grabbed him, praying to God with all my being to bring him back to me, and gave him mouth-to-mouth resuscitation all the way to the emergency hospital, bringing him back to life for but a moment.

Tragically, he didn't survive the night as he had lost too much oxygen and was already weakened from elder health issues. This was not the way I had wanted my first dog to pass. I had worked hard, earning straight A's every year of high school to get him. He was the love of my life and letting go of him seemed impossible. I wanted to die that night with him. To this day, I still relive that nightmare, wishing I had stuck to my boundaries and not let X intimidate me into listening to something so meaningless compared to the life of my dogs.

This is what a CNP does. Any boundaries you try to have with them will be shut down, including simple ones such as asking them to wait a couple of minutes so you can finish what you are doing. I had to learn the hard way to be firm on my boundaries. Later into our marriage, my resolve strengthened against him as hope for our relationship working out diminished. The more boundaries I stuck to, the less X was willing to stay in our marriage. Though his discard was long and painful, I am still grateful to have escaped the loveless marriage I was in.

If a CNP ignores your boundaries, they will insist you don't cross their own. Thus, the frustrating double-standard of a relationship with a CNP.

## Obsession with Superficial Things (Looks, Social Media)

We all love something superficial, whether it be getting our hair done, buying fancy new shoes, or posting on social media. However, watch out for someone who prioritizes superficialities over anything meaningful. For some people, social media is important to them as it is their career. While that's fine, especially with how attuned people are to the internet nowadays, there are still some red flags to look out for.

Be wary of those who exorbitantly flaunt their relationship online, prioritize good content over the feelings of others, use their influence to gain no matter the cost, and whose sole focus is attaining more money. These people are interested in themselves and what people can do for them. If you look at many top social media stars, their relationship life ends in turmoil, with the non-toxic person hurt and silenced while the social media influencer remains on top.

CNP parents will tear their children's self-esteem down, telling them they aren't good enough, that they should change their hair, lose or gain weight, dress better, etc. These negative comments about a child's appearance affect them mentally. CNP parents can do a lot of damage to their children in the long run.

If you notice your parent tearing you down this way, it is important to realize that it is not your fault and that you don't owe anything to those who tell you to change. The CNP parent gets supply from the misery of their child. When they insult their child's appearance, they're actually trying to conceal their envy. They feel jealous because inside, they are as self-conscious and self-loathing as they want to make their child feel.

My CNP ex was not publicly obsessed with materialistic things or social media, but he made sure he was included in photos, and if not, he'd guilt you into posting his photo. However, X barely posted on his own social media. He wanted to show the appearance of a happy family and that he was a loving family man, which couldn't be further from the truth. He was infatuated with porn and alcohol, which, when placed above other people, is also superficial. He drank in his office every night, all by himself, buying cases of beer, cognac, vodka, and whiskey. We had a fridge in the garage for any overflow, and nothing fit as it was jam-packed with his beers.

When he drank, he had a two-beer minimum before he'd get an inkling of a sense of humor, although his humor was awkward and strange. He wasn't funny, but you had to laugh, or he'd get offended. He was a sloppy and obnoxious drunk, his true narcissistic qualities exposed for that time. He talked endlessly about himself, slurring his words, laughing loudly in such a way you could tell just how fake he was, blatantly love-bombed those around him, slamming drinks on the table, and talking as loud as he could. He didn't care who was around him or if he was making anyone uncomfortable. It was simply his world, and we just existed in it.

He was also what I called a "marathon masturbator." While I don't see masturbating as wrong in the slightest, I couldn't believe how much he did it. He'd lock the door of his office and pleasured himself with porn nightly, though he never shared what exactly he watched. It bothered me when he would stay up late and come into our bedroom loudly, waking me up and picking a fight when I was half asleep.

The way a CNP approaches their superficial obsession is self-centered. They want all the attention to be on them, whether by actively demanding it as X did when drunk, disrupting their partner due to their activities, creating fights and drama online for attention, or fixating solely on looks. When considering whether your partner utilizes this emotional abuse tactic, consider whether they have a hyper-fixation on something superficial and whether that obsession

111

affects you or others. While it is easy to get swept up in superficialities, it becomes problematic when that fixation hurts and emotionally abuses other people.

## Stonewalling

Stonewalling is similar to and a form of the silent treatment. It occurs when a person turns away from the conversation or discussion, refusing to acknowledge or address the other person's concerns. They may ignore the pleas of the other person, dismiss them entirely, devalue the other person's argument, speak evasively, or invalidate the other's feelings. The conversation is completely shut down, leaving conflict unsolved and festering. This behavior causes the victim to feel anxious, isolated, depressed, and insignificant. Over time, stonewalling can drive a person mad from the abysmal feelings of hurt and confusion.

X often stonewalled during our arguments by walking out of the room before we could come to an agreement or solution or ignoring me as if I weren't there. It made me feel unheard and more frustrated. I became wound up to the point of yelling to be heard, which made the situation worse.

Stonewalling tells the victim they aren't worth responding to, their feelings are of minor importance, or they do not matter. It's horrible to put someone through and very emotionally damaging.

You may be surprised by how many different emotional abuse tactics exist and more shocked to learn that most CNPs utilize all of them! The most important thing you can do to arm yourself against the lethal venom of a CNP is to be aware of when any of these abuses are used against you. I wish I had been prepared going into my relationship so I could recognize that the problem was not with me but with him instead. Now, I hope the knowledge I've shared about emotional abuse will save you from a future of pain and frenzy.

## Feigned Ignorance

Feigned Ignorance is as it sounds. CNPs will play dumb about what they did, shifting the narrative to appear blameless. They will act as though they had no idea what they were doing and had no intention to hurt anyone, avoiding any accountability whatsoever. They may paint you as the villain for accusing them of having ill intentions. It is an effective tactic for manipulating the person who confronts the CNP into feeling doubtful about the legitimacy of the issue they spoke up about.

CNPs have made up excuses for everything. They especially feign ignorance when they have their backs up against the wall. They will chalk their behavior up to either not knowing better or simply not remembering they acted that way. My ex, however, opted to highlight the one confronting him as the bad guy rather than taking responsibility for his mistreatment. With my eldest daughter, who is not afraid to call him out on his behavior, X has feigned ignorance multiple times. He would act utterly shocked that she would dare suggest his actions were harmful or abusive. When she continued to press the issue, he would say he was disgusted by how she spoke to him and felt betrayed by her words when all he had ever shown her was love.

When my youngest confronted him in the past, he would ask her if this was coming from her feelings or from "your mother." Or he would compare her to me, telling her she sounds like "her mother," as if that was the worst thing she could ever do. He never once accepted that he was in the wrong. Instead, he painted his "accusers" as the bad guys. This often occurs in society with victims of domestic abuse and sexual assault. Survivors are "victim-blamed" when they tell their stories. People ask them why they didn't fight back, why they never left, why they put themselves in that situation, to begin with, etc. Or they blame the assault on what the person was wearing! All of this puts the interest back on what the victim did wrong in the scenario. It takes any negative attention away from the actual perpetrators, letting them walk away blameless.

Another example of feigned ignorance occurred during our divorce when X acted as though he didn't know much about investing, telling the court that I was the better investor than him. It was all an act of making himself look poor to the court while I appeared to be the wealthy one. X, who had millions of dollars in his paychecks and investments, wanted to get spousal support from me, who had next to nothing! X also feigned ignorance multiple times when confronted by

114

police for domestic violence by acting confused and innocent, then flipping the story so that I would appear as the out-of-control, abusive individual. The police believed him, not allowing me to get a word in to explain the truth, regardless of the physical marks on my body. When I told my parents or friends about his behavior, they would just say he was absentminded. However, that wasn't the true picture, just how he made others perceive him to be.

Feigned ignorance is very clever and harmful as it lowers the guard of the person it is directed toward. When someone seems confused or unknowledgeable about an issue another has attempted to bring up, it creates confusion in the other person, leading them to doubt the viability of their point. CNPs act naive and pretend they didn't know what they were doing nor how it was affecting you when, in reality, they are controlling you and using feigned ignorance to shield them from any blame. It works in their favor because people assume that the CNP is not intelligent enough to abuse. Feigned ignorance allows CNPs to slip back into the shadows and continue their harmful work.

## Illeism

Illeism is a unique trait for someone with narcissistic personality disorder. Not much research about illeism has been connected to narcissism. But, from my experience and hearing stories of other survivors of narcissistic abuse, I've learned it is a common trait that many Coverts or CNP personality types share. You may be wondering, what is illeism and what does it have to do with narcissism? In its most basic definition, illeism is the act of referring to oneself in the third person. We've seen this utilized in film, television, and books, but it is usually a strange phenomenon for someone to talk in the third person consistently. Hence, why most don't.

However, CNPs perform illeism quite regularly, especially when conveying words of genuine emotion. Because they do not feel the authentic connection of human love and affection as we do, when they say express words of love to you, many CNPs will separate themselves from those words, speaking in the third person as opposed to the first person. Thus, they aren't honestly expressing love to you. It is also done when the CNP feels defensive about protecting their image. Seem confusing? Here's an example.

Every evening, past midnight, X texts our daughters, "Good night. Daddy loves you." Not only does he text it late to disrupt their sleep schedules, but he never says, "I love you." It is a way to separate himself from honestly declaring love, for he feels no such affection. His good night texts are performative in nature, so he may appear the loving father without having to follow through. Indeed, his assertion of love reflects how he was as a parent: distant, removed, and unloving. X continues to use illeism to dissociate from being a real father and from being emotionally present to his children.

By referring to oneself in the third person, the CNP may, once again, shirk accountability for their lack of sentiment by simply treating themselves as if they are another person entirely. It is easier for them to express emotions they don't feel nor understand because they do not have to accept that feeling as their own. "Daddy loves you" could be any daddy who loves you or a word without meaning. When someone uses "I" to express an emotion, they fully claim that sentiment as their own. A CNP doesn't have to claim any feeling by using illeism.

It also works for a CNP as another great tool to devalue their victim. When they refer to themselves in the third person, the person they have targeted subconsciously does not feel the authenticity behind their words. This causes the victim to feel insecure and unloved, wondering why the CNP won't communicate their feelings as they do. Words of affirmation spoken in the third person are words with no interest in the life of the person they are directed towards.

Illeism is additionally used as a form of gaslighting. When a CNP speaks in the third person, it sounds as if someone else is making that statement other than the CNP. Therefore, if their specific words are quoted, people may not realize the CNP was talking about themselves. Instead, they will think another person believes it to be true of the CNP. For example, if the CNP says or primarily writes, "X is great," those who don't know the CNP is referring to him or herself will subconsciously begin to agree. They are planting their self-proclaimed "brilliance" into others' minds. With a larger group of people, a herd mentality occasionally takes form. We tend to agree with the majority's beliefs, despite the facts not being entirely there. Illeism is another form of subtle brainwashing. CNPs employ illeism to convince others that their lies are facts by frequently repeating them. Speaking in the third person helps their lies gain greater prominence.

If a CNP does not feel they are receiving enough praise or attention, they will utilize illeism to commend themselves and reinforce that whatever they do is worthy of notice.

If you notice a CNP or toxic individual in the third person, a technique you can use to call them out subtly is to respond in the second person, essentially agreeing that *the CNP* feels that way. Referring to my example with, "Daddy loves you." You may respond with, "Oh, you love me?" This lets them know that you took note of their usage of the third person while subtly forcing them to use the first person in response. However, this could end up enraging the CNP, who does not enjoy being called out, so use at your discretion. The best thing to do with a CNP is to go, of course, No Contact.

There are so many different emotional abuse tactics, and I wanted to capture all of them in this chapter to help you be aware of the many weapons CNPs will use against you. Emotional abuse is rampant in our society and skillfully wielded by CNPs. The way to fight it is to educate yourself on all the different tactics. This way, when one of those methods is used on you, you can properly identify it and avoid being manipulated by the toxic individual.

## Chapter 3: Dating a Covert, Narcissistic Psychopath

In Chapter 2, "Emotional Abuse," I wrote briefly about my first date with X. I stopped at the part where I had initially felt devalued. However, that was not the worst part of the date. In truth, the entire first date was quite a disaster. Yet, I unwarily entered a relationship with him. This is what distinguishes a terrible date with a non-CNP and a terrible date with a covert narcissist or CNP. Someone adept at covert manipulation will be able to pull you back in for that second date, third date, and then eventually a "serious" relationship.

Continuing with my first date story, we have already begun to see how persuasive X could be. Already, he had gotten me alone from the rest of the group when we bought tickets too early. Once the movie was over, I was looking forward to reconnecting with my brother and his friends afterward. Unfortunately, their movie ended later, and X didn't want to wait for it to be finished. Instead, he urged me to continue our date, saying he wanted to take me somewhere special. I felt excited by the idea of such romanticism...until I saw where we had arrived. It was a seedy bar that X claimed had "character." The floor was covered in peanut shells and various debris. The walls displayed memorabilia of motorcycle gangs and random clutter.

Forcing myself to keep an open mind, despite feeling out of place and uncomfortable, I let myself find peace in the song playing in the bar. It was "Unchained Melody," one of my favorite songs at the time.

After expressing how much I loved that song, X asked, "would you like to dance, my brown-eyed girl?"

At that moment, my current discomfort was replaced by his flattery. He'd noticed my eyes which made me feel special. When we danced to the song, I felt connected and cared for. He brought me close to him and cradled me gently while we danced. Not too close to where it felt too forward and not distant to where it felt awkward. It seemed just right. He was much taller than I was, and I felt safe and comforted in his arms, especially while still leery of my surroundings.

All the past struggles in our date simply melted away. However, when the song ended, I was wrenched back to reality. The reality I wished I'd paid more attention to.

X noticed a tow truck out front towing cars. He grabbed me by the arm and said we needed to rush out and get his car before they towed it away. Although we couldn't move it in time, X immediately flagged down the tow truck driver, asking if we could hitch a ride to the impound station with them. Here we were, in the middle of the night, hopping into a tow truck with a sketchy-looking guy. How romantic.

The guy yelled to get in fast as he didn't want to get beat up by angry customers. Rather than helping me into this big truck, X jumped in and pulled me up fast, slamming the truck door with his full strength on my thumb as I balanced myself in the doorway to climb into the cab. Though my thumb was throbbing in utter agony, and I was scared, I still tried to hold back the tears welling up in my eyes. X asked the tow truck driver if he could stop off at an ATM and a 7-eleven to get money for the impound fee and ice for my injured hand. The fact that X cared at that moment that my thumb needed ice made me feel thought of yet again, which detracted from what happened just prior. When we got to the ATM, X didn't have enough funds in his account and asked if I could cover him, promising to pay me back. I just wanted to get home, so I pulled out the money and gave it to him. He never ended up paying me back.

We collected his car at the impound, and he drove me back to where my car was parked at my brother's place. Once there, he pulled out the infamous narcissistic love-bombing technique, complimenting my eyes again and noting how impressed he was with how I handled the tow truck situation. Once again, my negative feelings dissipated as he made me feel cared about and proud of how I'd made it through such an ordeal. At the time, it was past one in the morning. I hadn't planned to stay out that late, but he moved closer, and we kissed for a little bit. Then, my brother interrupted, banging on the window and yelling at me to get home as our mother was worried. I was 22 years old, irritated, and embarrassed by my brother, so I told him F-off and go back to his place as I was leaving soon.

For the second time, X conveyed how impressed he was and said I was someone he wanted to marry. Hint! Big red flag. Someone who introduces the idea of marriage on the first date does not have good intentions. It merely suggests the idea of commitment in a relationship without any action behind it. It is like the magician claiming to have found a coin in your ear when there never was any coin other than the one the magician carries around to enchant different people with each new day.

Still, his admiration was short-lived. X continued to say that he doesn't date women as young as I was and that it probably wouldn't work out for us. Dumbfounded and upset by this sudden change, I found myself trying to prove to him that I was someone worthy enough to date. After such a terrible first date, most women would have never wanted to go out with the guy again. However, X made me feel he was someone everyone should be vying after. I felt devalued by his belief that I wasn't suitable for him because I was younger, which somehow made him more mature than me. Suddenly, it was as if I was auditioning for a part in his movie, though all his movies were rated extremely low on *Rotten Tomatoes*.

Since I was young and lacked relationship experience, I didn't know what to look out for. Therefore, I took X's words as a challenge and continued to date him. The dates did not get any better. On our third date, he invited me out with a group of his friends, mostly couples. Once again, it was at a pub. I wasn't a drinker, but he and his friends enjoyed getting stupid drunk together. At first, I thought it was comical and adapted to his needs. However, X was entirely ignorant of my needs. When we entered the pub, he immediately sat down with his friends, his back turned to me, leaving me to stand behind him awkwardly with no chairs available. He didn't make room for me, and one of his friends had to ask if they could find me a chair for everyone to scoot over to fit me in. I felt low at that moment and angry in a way I had never been before. Later, when we left, I lightly roundhouse kicked him on his buttocks.

X whipped around furiously and yelled, "F- me!"

I shrunk, embarrassed, and muttered softly, "You should know."

I wanted to hide and worried that we were over. During the car ride home, there was a long stretch of silence, followed by a condescending lecture about how I behaved wrongly. I felt terrible and apologized profusely, not knowing what came over me. We were both martial artists, so I had felt it was a good swift kick in the pants to say, "Hey, please notice me and don't treat me so poorly ever again!" I knew it was wrong and very uncharacteristic, so I felt very guilty. I couldn't figure out why I'd felt so reactive at that moment.

Although I'd reacted inappropriately, he made no mention of the way he'd ignored me with his friends. The focus was all on my bad reaction. I thought he'd laugh that I roundhouse kicked him in the butt because it wasn't as if I'd hurt him, considering he was much bigger than me. The problem was that I had hurt his ego, which was not allowed.

As you can see, dating a CNP is not entirely romantic. Nevertheless, it is clouded over by love-bombing. CNPs will praise you, say you're their soulmate, and buy you extravagant gifts while getting away with threatening and disrespecting you. One of the ways you can figure out whether the person you are dating is toxic is by looking at your own behavior. Don't be critical of how you acted. Instead, observe and try to figure out why you reacted a certain way. Suppose you aren't usually a reactive person, or you've noticed that you've begun acting differently since starting the relationship. In that case, you are likely feeling some neglect or frustration with your partner. A healthy relationship brings out the best in you, and a great partner sees your value as a human being. In contrast, a toxic relationship morphs you into someone you don't recognize and carves self-doubt into your mind.

While you're still in the dating part of a relationship, try to examine your dates and the time spent with the other person. Think about why you want to go on a date with them again. Was it something they *said* or *did* that made you feel good? In my experience, words are just that: words. Actions reveal the truth about an individual. If the person's conduct made you feel good, included, and cared for, continue pursuing a relationship. However, if their *actions* were off-putting, detached, or unpleasant, but their *words* sounded loving, you should reconsider continuing that relationship.

After all, the deadliest poisons can be concealed with a bit of sugar.

## Chapter 4: The Wedding Trap

Marriage to a CNP is the opposite of a fairytale. It's a psychological horror show complete with a tragic ending in which the victim of narcissistic abuse is left with emotional scars and an uncertain future. Unfortunately, marriage is the ultimate trap the CNP hopes to set. It keeps their victims locked in as one person struggles to keep the relationship together while the CNP enjoys the feeling of control and power they receive from their partner's struggle.

Narcissists get married because they need a constant source of supply. They see their spouse not as a companion but as a housemaid, sex partner, cook, and tool for their toolbox. They want the parent they never had, not a person to grow and share responsibilities with. Marriage to a CNP will throw you into the horror story version of Cinderella. You signed a contract for servitude, abuse, and manipulation, not love or understanding. Once that marriage contract is signed, the marriage responsibilities land on your shoulder while they enjoy a double life behind your back. Marriage allows CNPs to insult, blame shift, and project their insecurities onto their partner without needing to take accountability. It becomes much more difficult to leave a CNP when you are married to one, and they know that.

I will share the story of my marriage with a covert, narcissistic psychopath in hopes of showing those who have gone through a similar experience that they are not alone and caution others about the dangers of marrying a CNP.

My marriage had a rocky start, though I didn't put the pieces together at the time. Usually, people remember their wedding proposal as something happy and romantic. To me, it felt a bit disappointing. Holidays are especially appealing to the CNP to tarnish. Mine started on Christmas night, surrounded by my family. X left me clues leading to an area in my home. We were all confident that he was leading up to the marriage proposal. I was so excited. I wanted badly to get married to the man I loved. When I reached the final clue and saw that it was in a ring box, I was sure this was the moment he would propose. My family and I were elated, and I felt swept up in the idea of how romantic the scavenger hunt he put together was. However, when I opened the box, there was a familiar key inside instead of a ring. It was a key to our outdoor storage shed. Everyone was confused but still optimistic, thinking he set something special up there to propose to me. We all went out to the backyard shed, and I opened the lock while my family eagerly watched behind me to see X's proposal. Instead of a proposal, the surprise was a canoe.

I had expressed interest in canoeing as I knew X was passionate about it and wanted to share that activity. Though I was delighted to have my canoe, I couldn't help feeling a tinge of disappointment as I had thought maybe my family's feelings were right and X was going to be there to propose to me. It was an embarrassment in front of my family, who had been expecting a romantic marriage proposal, only to be blindsided by something wholly different. Although everyone was baffled and slightly disappointed by the misleading ring box, how could we be upset? After all, there was a beautiful new blue canoe for me.

The next day, X tied a ring to my dog and proposed. I was excited to marry him and didn't hesitate to say yes, but I couldn't help feeling something off about the proposal. The day before had been so romantic, and the next day didn't compare. It was sweet that he put the ring on the dog and proposed that way, but it lost its romantic effect for me. I couldn't figure out why I felt that way, but there was no way I could bring it up to X, who had been so sweet to buy me a canoe and had just proposed to me with no family around to celebrate it.

I thought perhaps I was being ungrateful, but now I know that wasn't it. CNPs don't like to make their partners feel special when it counts. The day he gave me the canoe and used a ring box as one of the clue holders, he knew what that meant. The ring box was a big hint that he was proposing. And yet, he didn't. My whole family was there with me, and it would have been the perfect moment to propose, but he waited until the next day when I was alone. It felt a bit isolating as I had thought I would share that special moment with everyone I cared for. Still, I knew I loved X and wanted to marry him, so I pushed away my thoughts about the proposal and focused on making the wedding day as perfect as can be.

Just before our wedding, my illness took a turn for the worse. I was at a karate tournament, and nausea hit for the first time in the ring. I thought it would go away and attended a party afterward for X's job, but I had to return to the hotel we were staying at. The next day, we

127

were supposed to pick up our engagement rings, and I found myself looking at every trash can to be sick in. I almost called off the wedding, something X seemed fine with, which I thought was strange at the time but still overlooked. Still, I went through with it.

I don't know how I managed to make it through our wedding. It was supposed to be a dream wedding, and I had planned it out to the T. While everyone else enjoyed the wedding, my debilitating stomach pain and nausea kept me anxious and unable to eat the entire time. Still, I managed to enjoy the wedding, though I nearly fainted as I finished a dance with X's stepfather. However, our honeymoon was a different story.

I felt sicker than I'd ever felt, which X attributed to nerves. We were supposed to have a beautiful vacation in Hawaii, but I could barely get to the beach because I was so sick. It felt like a tease, being surrounded by such beauty but caged by my own body. I felt bad for X at the time, but he still managed to see most of the island on his own. I went out with him once, only to spend the time dry heaving into a plastic bag in the car. I felt humiliated and didn't know why I was suffering so dreadfully. We left Hawaii earlier than planned, and I've been battling nausea. Most married couples look back on their honeymoon with joy, but when I think of my honeymoon, I remember the trauma of the stomach pain and nausea I suffered.

After our honeymoon, X continued working and traveling while I struggled with my health. He was absent most of the time, which left me feeling quite lonely. X began pushing his desire to have children on me as soon as we married. He would point out babies to me, make subtle comments about wanting to have children, and repeatedly said he saw his life with children. We had this discussion before marriage as well. I was young, twenty-three, and barely starting my adult life. X stated our relationship was not worth continuing if I could not guarantee children. I should have walked away at once. If our relationship was not worthwhile enough for him without children, how would it be any different with children? Yet, this thought never entered my mind in the heat of the moment. I felt that I had invested so much time and love into him that I didn't want to end it all based on something I wasn't sure about. I knew then that I did not want children so early on in my life, but what if, eventually, I would? What if my maternal clock was simply late?

Now that we were married, X immediately became more persistent about having children. We had barely been married a year, and X told me that if we did not have kids, he didn't see our marriage working and that we should get a divorce. I was mortified at such a direct, heartless, cold statement. The ink was barely dry on the marriage contract; I'd just taken an oath of love, for better or worse, in sickness and health. I couldn't fathom getting a divorce so early into our marriage. I didn't believe in divorce, and X knew where I stood on that issue. We agreed we'd work our differences out together. How could he dismiss all that as if it were never discussed and make such a blatant threat? I was afraid to have children as I had been diagnosed with Endometriosis which was progressively worsening. I didn't want to have children when I felt so unwell. With the looming threat of divorce on my mind, another shock came my way. My father had a massive heart attack and almost died. I realized how short life can be and how it can all change in an instant. I wanted to give my father grandchildren. I told him in the hospital that I would start trying for children if he lived. I didn't want him to miss that opportunity and felt under a lot of pressure with the fear of divorce and losing my father. And so, with my decision finalized, we began trying to conceive.

What I didn't know then was that I had a duty to myself and my own mental and physical health. I did not owe my husband children, especially so early in our marriage, if I did not feel ready for them. And while I do not regret my decision to have kids, I wish it had been made from love and mutual respect rather than an all-or-nothing demand from X and at a vulnerable, emotional time when my father's life was at risk. However, I am blessed to have my children and happy that my father could be a part of their lives.

Growing up, I was raised on the idea of a fairytale romance. Furthermore, I had no experience with the idea of an abusive marriage, as my parents showed love and respect to one another in their relationship. My father, especially, was a doting and caring husband to my mother, even when she didn't quite deserve it. Therefore, I expected making love with the person I married would be something enjoyable and passionate, as the books and movies portrayed it to be. It was supposed to be an equal union between two loving partners. I didn't know intimate relations with a CNP are not about both partners. Instead, it solely focuses on the CNP partner's enjoyment.

Sex for me was painful, mainly because I was suffering from Endometriosis. And yet, X didn't do anything to make it less uncomfortable. He told me the things he wanted me to do that would make him feel pleasure but did not try to find out what made me feel good. The truth is, I was very inexperienced in sex and didn't know what would please me. X didn't care to find out or explore that with me. I felt like a tool to be used for his enjoyment. When we had sex, I didn't feel loved at all. And when I didn't want to have sex, X would covertly try to pressure me to change my mind. He would guilt-trip me into intimacy, saying that I was obligated not to deprive him of his primal needs as his wife.

In our twenty-seven years of marriage, we very rarely had sex. None of those times were enjoyable for me whatsoever. Most of the time, it felt like rape. When a person is pressured into having sex through manipulation, there is no authentic consent or connection.

Moving forward, I was overjoyed when my first daughter was born. My motherly love for her kicked in instantly. I thought that, since X wanted children so badly, he would step up and be there as a father. However, X was more distant and absent than ever, leaving me sick and taking care of our firstborn baby on my own. This was how X was as a father to both of our children. He was mostly away on "business" trips. The rare times he was home, he was hardly physically present and entirely emotionally uninvested, spending his time in so-called meetings in his office. Getting him to drive the girls to school and their activities was a burden, and he consistently made them arrive late. I would get calls from teachers complaining about their tardiness, yet there was nothing I could do about it as I was chronically ill and too sick to leave the restroom for a lengthy time.

I begged X to put more effort into being on time, printing out schedules with everything he needed to know. But, he still lacked care and responsibility. Life revolved around his schedule and what worked for him, not what worked for our family or daughters. As a father, he was not available enough, so I had to hire mother's helpers to take our girls to their activities. I was too sick and unable to leave home. My stomach was unpredictable, and my body reacted dangerously to any heightened emotions. At one point, I could not keep anything down and was hooked up to a PICC line that fed me through my veins. I would get into a state of Tetany in which my blood sugar was so low that I was partially paralyzed and trembling for hours. X witnessed this and knew it all, but he never fully believed it, though it was staring him in the face. He did not care about the danger my illness put our daughters and me, nor other drivers should I have pushed myself to drive.

Instead, he complained about how hiring helpers were a financial drain on his accounts. I didn't know what he expected me to do. Did he want me to fire the helper and not have the ability to get our girls to school? He wasn't around nor available to take them. It all made no sense to me, and the fact he blamed any loss of finances on me was disheartening. It led to many fights, which he often instigated in front of our children. I never wanted to fight in front of them, but X deliberately started fights, using word salad to confuse me and wind me up. Throughout my entire marriage, I was in a constant state of fight or flight. I was stressed and felt unheard and unappreciated. Though I had all these negative feelings, I never knew why I felt this way. I knew he was absent and didn't step up, but I couldn't figure out why he acted this way.

If I had known he was a CNP and that every action was deliberate, I feel I would have been able to handle it better. However, I still hung on to that hope that he would return to the person he was during the love-bombing stage of our relationship. I thought that once the kids were grown up, we would enjoy a relaxing retirement in the company of each other. That was what I had wanted for my elderly years, a companion to spend my days with. I didn't know that he already had retirement plans, and they had never included me.

In your relationship, you may wonder how a terrible marriage like this can last for so long and why. That is because marriage is the ultimate supply trap for the CNP. Normal and healthy individuals don't go into marriage hoping it will end. Most people will do everything possible to keep their union strong, especially with kids involved. CNPs take advantage of that desire. They may use divorce as a threat but won't go through with it until they feel they can get no more supply from you. Every fight, little argument, and constant disappointment was supply to X. He thrived off my pain.

CNPs will prolong marriage until they have completely stripped you of who you are. Most victims of narcissistic abuse feel as though they've lost themselves over the years. One of the most challenging parts of recovering from the trauma of such abuse is learning to find yourself again and love yourself too.

Once you get married to a CNP, it becomes infinitely more difficult to break out. That is why it is imperative to know and recognize the red flags before committing to a serious relationship with someone. However, if you find yourself in an emotionally abusive marriage, use the information you've learned about the CNP's abuse tactics to shield yourself from the abuse. Still, your best option is to get out of that marriage. A relationship with a CNP will never get better and will never change. It will be a cycle of love-bombing and abuse. Every time you feel you've moved a step forward, you simultaneously move two steps backward without realizing it. The wedding traps you, and once the narcissist knows they have you, their mask begins to fall off.

In order to avoid the torment of marrying a CNP, it is vital to discuss bills, parenting styles, credit and debt, religion, what beliefs will be instilled in your children, traumas, sexual expectations, financial responsibilities, family health history, mental health history, goals, careers, education, political views, and anything else you believe is important in a marriage. Love is not enough to keep a marriage strong. You need the fundamentals as well. If your partner isn't willing to have an honest discussion with you about those points, the marriage is likely to struggle and eventually fail.

## Chapter 5: Mask Removed

A narcissist will rarely remove their mask, and they only reveal their true, evil nature to the person they're abusing. Unfortunately for me, my CNP removed his mask, and it was a night forever stained in my mind.

I was helping my youngest daughter with homework she was struggling with. After exhausting all my resources, I asked if X could come out of his office to help. I smelled the potent odor of alcohol on his breath, and he'd appeared bothered to have been asked to leave his computer, though it was after typical working hours and dinner. X made homework explanations much more complicated than needed, and my daughter struggled to understand him. X lost his temper and grabbed her heavy textbook, throwing the book across the room.

Concerned, I told X that was not the kind of help I asked for and let him know he could've hurt our daughter if that book had hit her. After all, it had flown quite close to her head. I picked up the book and attempted to get her re-focused. X was still adamant that he stay and help, so we continued the lesson. My daughter and I had been joking together, trying to make the learning experience more fun. She was trying to recall the information and made a silly error, so I tapped her lightly on the noggin with the eraser of a pencil, reminding her that she knew the answer, to which she laughed and answered it correctly. X glared at me, his eyes suddenly intense.

He pointed his finger at me and said, "don't ever do that again."

I still felt playful and tapped X on the head, very lightly, as I had done with my daughter, to show him that there was no malicious intent. Big mistake. He knocked my arm back so hard the pencil flew from it. I was in shock. Did that just happen?

Then, he told my daughter, "You want to see what really bugs Mom?"

X took his open hand and slammed me on the top of my head as hard as he could. I immediately went into fight or flight, feeling my life was in danger. I punched back to get him away from me, and he shoved me hard. My body flew back through the kitchen chairs, causing me to trip and fall into the wood and metal dog crates in the kitchen. My youngest daughter began crying, horrified at what she'd just witnessed. I picked up a chair to defend myself, and he picked one up, ready to throw it at me! My heart stopped; I was out of breath, unable to comprehend how this demon had suddenly appeared. The ultimate female degradation was happening to me in front of our child. What was I teaching her now? When I glanced at my daughter and saw the terror in her eyes, I knew this had to stop. I put the chair down and ran to call 911.

X immediately headed out the front door, but as soon as he heard me describe his attire and car, he hesitated. Instead, X called his friend and immediately gathered our youngest daughter upstairs to wait until the police arrived. X brought our daughters into the same room to tell them what to say to the police if they were questioned. He was grooming them to defend him. Too terrified to follow, I called my mom and waited on the phone until the police arrived but yelled at him not to put a hand on our girls. Luckily, he did not.

When the police arrived, X's story was extravagant to the point that the police laughed when they came to discuss it with me. I was trembling in fear after being brutalized in front of our children, and they were laughing. *What about all this was funny* kept circling in the back of my mind as I tried to control the physical pain and Tetany that began consuming my body. The officer explained that X claimed I was having a high from eating chocolate and came after him aggressively. I could tell they were having a hard time believing his story, but still, they were unhelpful. As discussed in Chapter 2, using nonsensical words or arguments is word salad. X's logic that I was on a "chocolate high" was, indeed, word salad. Obviously, it made no sense. However, his goal was to distract the police from his actions and make the situation more confusing.

Because I had hit back in self-defense, the police told me that if I filed charges, X would also, and both of our girls' parents would be taken away. They stated that this would probably be a one-time incident since we had many years of marriage together, and this was the first time any physical abuse had occurred. Little did I know there was plenty of physical abuse covered up by what X called reflexes or unintentional accidents.

It was just before the holidays, and my oldest, standing at the top of our stairs, looked down and cried, "don't put daddy in jail, mommy!"

I wondered how she knew he could go to jail. What had he been filling her head up in the moments prior to the police arriving? My oldest wasn't present during his brutality, only my youngest, who was shaken up from what she had just seen with her own eyes. I didn't want the girls to lose both of their parents, or their father, right before Christmas, so I did not press charges.

When the officers spoke to me, I had an intense bodily reaction due to the stress of the night. My arms filled with electricity, becoming partially paralyzed. My thumbs and pinkies turned inwards, touching each other. I couldn't spread my fingers apart or feel my arms. The intensity of sparks going up and down my arms and one of my legs was unlike anything I'd ever experienced. It's difficult to describe Tetany, but it is truly a more than unsettling feeling. The officers were concerned and advised that I take an ambulance to the hospital. I could not leave my children with what I felt was a dangerous man in his current state of mind and alcohol consumption. I said it would probably pass, but I had no idea what it was at the time.

When the officers left, I had no choice but to leave my daughters in the care of their father while I became sick to my stomach in the restroom, lying and sobbing in pain near the toilet on the floor, worried about my daughters if they were safe downstairs with what I felt was a monster. After consulting my doctor the following day, he diagnosed the symptoms I was experiencing as Tetany. It lasted another hour or so and would become another unpredictable symptom in my health struggles.

It was one of the worst nights of my life. Never had I thought X would lay a hand on me deliberately. Though I knew he was a mostly absent father and emotionally unavailable husband, I never knew the extent of abuse X would reach. That's the danger of the CNP; you never know when they might snap and seriously hurt you.

Later, I found out that during that time, X had been trying to reconnect with his estranged paternal father, who had abandoned and, by X's word of mouth, abused him as a child. However, I found out when he revealed it during our "apology session." My father suggested we talk out what happened that night to see if we could come to any resolution and repair the fractured relationship that his abuse brought. I felt what had occurred was too much for a simple apology to cover. Still, X was in the Hoover phase of the cycle, determined to get his supply back. He never took full accountability for his actions, instead attributing his violent behavior to finding out that his biological father wanted nothing to do with him. Had I known before, I would have empathized with him much more. However, in that moment, I saw through the reason why he told me. He was using it as an easy way to get back in my good graces.

I had no knowledge of him trying to reconnect with his father before the incident, as he had a history of hiding anything personal from me. He never let me open his mail, never shared our financials with me, and was very secretive. A couple of nights prior, I noted the amount of alcohol X was consuming. He'd purchased quite a bit of hard liquors and a suspiciously large amount of beer for one person. He did not have friends over for a drinking night but went through the bottles of alcohol alone. Alcohol and CNPs are a dangerous combination as it brings out a darker side to them, just as it did with X. Since he only revealed his personal struggles when in the limelight of the previous night's event, it felt insincere as if he were trying to excuse his physical abuse.

At that point, I felt no hope left for my marriage ever getting better and no hope for X being the person I thought he was when I'd met him. I wanted to keep the family together to provide security and a family for my girls. Divorcing with my young children would create further trauma with custody issues and the heightened emotions of divorce. If he showed signs of becoming violent to the point where it was unsafe for us to live with him, I would have left him immediately. Still, I believed the police's words that this would not be a reoccurring event. For the most part, they had been correct. We did not have an overt incident like this one again. However, X was never a gentle person, and I knew not to push him for fear that the monster beneath his mask would be unveiled again. I had to modify my behavior around him, continually walking on eggshells. People who must walk on eggshells around their partner are hyper-vigilant about not upsetting them. If you notice that you constantly have to subdue your personality to appease your partner, this is a form of their control over you. Eventually, the parts you like most about yourself will be erased by the CNP, leaving you a shell of the person you once were.

Still, several other instances of physical abuse were covertly covered up by believable untruths. The first happened when X bruised my nose while demonstrating what he learned from his Tae Kwon Do training. If you can recall from the earlier chapter, he claimed my injury was caused by the technique's effectivity, not the sheer brutality of his force. Before X, I dated a martial artist and competed as one.

Unless we intentionally meant to cause harm, we could control our movements, especially from learning how to spar safely. If you went too far while competing, you'd get a warning or be disqualified from the match. Though I believed his lie at the time, I realized later that this was the first instance of physical abuse because it truly wasn't an accident.

While dating, if I accidentally grazed his private parts, he'd explode in rage and push me hard to the ground. When I questioned that behavior, he'd say I didn't realize just how painful getting knocked in the gonads is and that I need to be more careful not to harm in. X claimed his reaction was a normal reflex to pain. Instead of realizing that his reaction to pain should not include harming others, I felt guilty and made sure to be careful of his man parts.

Another instance occurred while we were dating. My alarm was set the loudest as I've always been a deep sleeper. It went off, as usual, except X had spent the night. When the alarm sounded, he shot up so fast and went to punch me in the face. He stopped a tiny distance before making contact when I felt the air shift over me and asked him what he was doing. He justified his violent outburst by saying he was sensitive to loud noises and that, again, it was his reflex! I became scared of triggering his reflexes and modified my behavior to suit his needs.

Each of these events happened unexpectedly, with no warning, and at odd distant times, so I couldn't piece it together. Other covert, physical abuse occurred while we "playfully" sparred. Although it was meant to be a lighthearted and fun way to practice our skills, I'd get hurt. With my previous boyfriend, who was a blackbelt, our sparring ended in play and fun. I never once got hurt. I once socked him in his private parts hard on accident, and he fell to the ground in sheer agony. I felt horrible and comforted him, apologizing profusely. Once he could catch his breath again, he laughed and said it was okay. He knew it was an accident and saw my remorse, and of course, I was more careful going forward. In such a painful, emotionally straining moment, he never lashed out at me nor retaliated as we continued to spar and practice martial arts together.

I was excited to spar with X as I had done with others in my club, tournaments, and my past boyfriend. However, it was not fun. It hurt. Every kick he threw, he threw at me. Blocking his heavy, long, hairy legs would bruise my arms and legs. The pain intensity with each block or hit was too much to handle. Here I was, enjoying a mutual sport with someone I admired and had affection for, and I had to stop. I could not spar with him anymore. Something that should have been a mutual, fun activity became a negative, abusive one masked behind the art of the sport.

I can recall so many more instances of harm masked by the excuse of an accident or made-up reflex. Another time, we were in X's office joking and being playful. Then, out of the blue, he pushed me into another office chair, and I ended up bruised and on the floor in pain. Again, when I questioned him, he said it was just a reflex and not to be so sensitive and quick to pass judgment. Xlabeled every instance of physical abuse as nothing more than a reflex, accident, or effective martial art technique.

In the next chapter, I will go over what it is like to divorce a CNP in more detail, but for this chapter, I'd like to talk about another instance in which the full mask of my CNP ex fell off another time. It was during the divorce X secretly used our community funds and purchased another home behind my back as well as the courts. He had already stolen valuable financial documents, our computer servers, and storage drives. These items would have revealed to the judge how much money X had transferred between accounts, stolen, and hidden away. When I realized that, I quickly had the locks changed in the home. When X came over to take the rest of his belongings, he saw that the locksmith was changing the locks and reacted violently. Seeing me with the new key, he ran towards me, aiming to grab the key from my hands. I fled, and X chased me around the entire home, from the front yard to the backyard and back to the front again. The look on his face was pure malice as he pursued me. Terrified, I ran to the locksmith's vehicle as he pulled away from the driveway, begging him to let me in. Thankfully, the locksmith let me hide in his car and walked out to talk to X to calm him down. My lawyer advised me to call the police, and I did, but X called them too.

This time, the police believed X's story that I was unhinged. When they came to talk to me, they were condescending and unhelpful. I was holding a large fluorescent, orange pen the locksmith gave me as a marketing memento with the company number and info in my hand. I wanted to give it to the officers so they could call and get further information as he was a witness to the event. The officer told me to put the pen down because I could stab him! Keep in mind, I'm short and frail compared to the tall, armed officers. Somehow, X twisted the story so much that the police were threatened by a short woman with a toy-like ballpoint pen. Truly, it's impressive. I'm unsure if that says much about X's skills or less about the police officers.

These moments were not the only time X was physically abusive. Instead, they were the instances his mask came off to reveal the true monster inside of him. X chose to abuse deceptively. If X struck our kids or dogs for accidentally grazing his privates, which he was very protective of, he would once again say it was due to reflexes. His so-called love hurt. X would hug me so hard that my ribs would dislocate. His hugs did not feel loving. When I shrieked in pain, he'd make me feel guilty for not allowing him to show his affection. Another method X used was to flip the script back onto me. It was the last time I would ever accept a hug from him again. I later realized these "reflexes" or accidents were intentional and meant to confuse me. I would repeatedly get hurt by him and not understand why or how. X gaslighted me soon afterward by claiming he never hugged or struck that hard and that he had love and care for me. It's important to notice how easily they speak the words, but their actions sorely differ.

I cautioned our girls to be careful around daddy's private parts because he couldn't control his reflexes. The way he seemed out of control of his actions yet still hurt our children or me had been of concern to me. However, I didn't realize back then that the physical abuse from X was not overt like most abusers. Instead, he made his unseen so that we didn't realize it was happening. It was when I finally saw through his mask and when he made his abusive capabilities known that I realized it was a part of him. When he got angry, he had such a fierce look that drew fear into my heart. His narcissistic rage was uncontrolled, but at the same time, he managed to cover it. No one else knew it was intentional, and I would continuously second guess myself. When we divorced, I knew I had not been wrong and that I should have trusted my instincts.

When a CNP's mask is lifted, it can be terrifying as you will witness the true monster beneath. They almost seem inhuman, their eyes black, lacking souls. The mask can crack or slip off through rage or when they discard you. It's when they have no reason to charm you anymore or are done using you as their supply (for the moment) will their true nature be shown. However, it will be brief. Brief enough that you may doubt whether you saw it at all. Still, when you see that mask come off and their true nature, you must leave and go completely No Contact with them. There is no reasoning with them or fixing them. I had believed that my ex would get better and that his abuse was just a slip-up, but I was wrong. Abusers will do it again and again once they get away with it.

To safely escape, make sure you have a close confidant or family member to go to when you make your escape. Try not to alert them or say goodbye. It is better to be discreet as CNPs will lash out when they realize you are leaving them, rather than the other way around. If you're tempted to give them another chance, remember that there are no second chances when it comes to abuse. If they physically abuse you, they are also emotionally abusing you. They have run through all their second chances, perhaps without you realizing it.

Going No Contact with a CNP can be difficult, and the trauma of their abuse will be lasting. In Chapter Nine, we will discuss the healing process and how to regain your life after being with a covert, narcissistic psychopath. No matter how long or short the CNP has been in your life, they can still leave a lasting impact. Still, it is possible to move on and recover from their abuse.

## Chapter 6: The Golden Child and the Scapegoat

Narcissistic parents with two or more children typically have a golden child and a scapegoated child. The golden child is the child the narcissist favors most in the family. They will pick a favorite, whether the parent is an overt narcissist or a CNP. The golden child is usually the one who most resembles themselves or is more easily manipulated. They also may be the child that doesn't listen as much and making them the golden child hides the narcissist's inability to control them. The other child or children become the scapegoats or the ones they don't favor as much. They often make children feel less than the golden child through how they treat that child. The scapegoat is usually the child that is more independent in their thoughts, therefore threatening the narcissistic parent's self-esteem. Sometimes the roles of scapegoat and golden child can also be determined by other factors such as gender, age, or appearances.

It may be confusing why a parent would choose to separate their children between being the golden child and the scapegoat. The answer to that question is because the malignant narcissist, especially a CNP,wants a victim or source of stable narcissistic supply. They want to feel superior and in control at all times. By messing with the family dynamic and creating internal instability through the treatment of their children, the narcissist maintains that control. Both children will be either directly or indirectly vying for the narcissist's affection while the narcissist basks in the attention.

If the narcissist has chosen an enabling spouse, they have the utmost authority around the household. An enabling parent does not fight against the narcissist, enabling their toxic behavior instead. They may also turn against the scapegoat child and allow the abuse to continue. The narcissist will manipulate and use whatever means necessary to maintain their control. The other family members must follow their lead or be subject to their wrath.

The scapegoat can do nothing right in the eyes of the narcissistic parent. Anything that goes wrong in the family is blamed on the scapegoat child. They are often given the most responsibility and criticism in the family. The scapegoat lives under more restrictive rules that the golden child may not have to follow. For instance, the golden child may be able to hang out with their friends, but for the scapegoat, there is a reason they can't go out with friends, which is blamed on them. No matter how hard the scapegoat works to please their parents, they will never be good enough for the narcissistic parent.

There are a few types of narcissistic parents that scapegoat their children. Some overt narcissists are not malignant. Their behavior is still abusive to the children, and they pick favorites, but at the end of the day, they still love their children and will support them. Although it is not the healthiest upbringing, and their parenting style can set their child up for failure when they are older, their behaviors are not intentional. This type of narcissist is more on the mental illness side of the condition. They wound with words rather than actions.

My mother was this type of narcissist. She never supported anything I was passionate about and constantly brought me down.

However, she still did try to guide me and did love me. Though I have a stronger relationship with my father, I still have a strong relationship with my mother. She had always offered me a home to return to if I needed one, been a wonderful grandmother to my children, and given me her attention and empathy when I was very depressed or needed a shoulder to cry on. She would give her last dollar to help her family and never asked for anything in return. On the other hand, if she gave gifts to friends' kids and they didn't give back to hers, or worse, gave a gift she didn't appreciate, she would express her strong opinions about it and felt they were undeserving of her generosity. However, she was typically judgmental regarding non-important situations and not toward those who needed help.

When I learned about narcissistic personality disorder, I realized my mother's hurtful qualities were due to her narcissism. That's when I began setting boundaries for myself and her to avoid getting hurt further. I let myself step away from conversations going down a painful path and learned it was okay to say no to her though she didn't like it. I also began not letting her words affect me, brushing them off my shoulder instead. Whenever she said something hurtful, I didn't argue or try to reason with her. Instead, I expressed to her plainly that her words were unkind. If she persisted, I told her I would talk to her later. By maintaining these boundaries, I was able to have a good relationship with my mother.

On the other hand, the malignant overt narcissist is a different situation. Their words are meant to destroy, and if you try to set boundaries with them, they will tear them down with no remorse.

They will have something to say about anything or anyone the scapegoat child likes and will never hear reason. It is not possible to have a healthy bond with them as they are determined to break their child down so that they will feel better about themselves. Think of them as the mean girls or douchebags in a 2000s teen flick. To everyone else, they're the life of the party. But to their child, they are bullies. They have no qualms about tearing the scapegoat child down in front of other people, as long as it makes them or their golden child look good. They prefer people to look down on the scapegoat just as they do. That way, they can destroy the scapegoat's self-esteem further. The malignant narcissists are the type of parents you'll want to research the lowest-rated nursing homes on Yelp for (Just kidding...).

Another more sinister type of parent is the covert narcissist or CNP. They are just as malignant as the overt narcissistic parent but abuse more imperceptibly. All narcissistic parents condition the scapegoat to believe that how they are treated is the child's fault and that they deserve to be abused. On the other hand, CNPs gaslight the scapegoat by denying any mistreatment or abuse occurred. The golden child will get special treatment, more time spent with the narcissistic parent, constant praise, or won't get in trouble for the same thing a scapegoat child would get in trouble for. The CNP parent will also enable the golden child to treat the scapegoat wrongly or unfairly, so the other child feels left out and ganged up on.

For example, after the divorce, my daughter confided in me that X would favor our eldest when she went on long car rides with her father and sister. My daughter loves to read, but she can't focus on reading when people are talking or singing. Her sister would sing during the car rides, usually when my youngest tried to read or focus on homework. When she asked her sister to stop, and her sister refused to, she would get upset. Meanwhile, her father didn't intervene except to tell her to let her older sister sing. Back when they were younger, there were no phones to distract children on long car rides, and they were usually on their way to auditions in Los Angeles, a good couple of hours from where we lived. I can imagine how frustrating it would be to want to pass the time by reading a book or doing homework, only to be unable to do so.

Other times, her sister would push down the backrest of her car seat when her sister was behind her so she could take a nap lying down. She would push it down far enough that it made her younger sister feel uncomfortable. After all, having a car seat practically on your lap is not fun. Rather than telling her older sister to lift the front seat more, X told the complaining scapegoated younger sister to let her sleep instead. My youngest often slept uncomfortably in the car, resting her head on the window. She thought it was unfair that she had to put up with a seat on her legs so that her sister could be more comfortable. The problem wasn't moving the seat's backrest a bit down but that her older sister didn't seem to care that it was bothering her.

Worst of all, her father didn't appear to care either. Instead, he would scold her for complaining and let her sister do it anyway. X incessantly took her older sister's side whenever there were fights between the two siblings. I never found out about these issues until after the divorce. My daughter said she was worried I would bring it up to X. She had figured out well before me that there was no changing how X behaved. When my youngest had pointed out his favoritism in the past, he never changed his actions. Still, he would speak with her privately and make her feel guilty for believing he had favorites. She said he would tell her that he loved them both equally and didn't want her to think that way, but she could never place why she wanted that conversation to end so quickly. She would appease and say she believed him, but deep down, she never did.

That is because his words are never sincere nor backed by any actions. A deep conversation with X feels awkward and uncomfortable. It was more about him being the victim, and your needs for basic respect and care impacted his very existence. Although X was in the wrong, he made us feel like we were the ones to wrong him. With our younger daughter, he said her belief that he played favorites was untrue and hurt *his* feelings. This confused her, causing her to doubt whether it was all in her mind. Instead of coming to a resolution, X made her feel guilty about the entire situation. He never tried to find out why she felt that way or tried to fix the problem. Instead, he denied its truth, and love bombed.

With an overt narcissist, who the golden child and scapegoat are is often apparent. They may outright tell the scapegoat child that they should be more like their sibling or that they like their sibling more than them. However, a CNP does not show their cards so openly. They will play the part of the loving parent of both children, either through social media or spoken words, but when it matters, they pick a side. It is very emotionally damaging when the parent doesn't choose the scapegoat, whether they are in the right or have done something exceptional.

A CNP will make the golden child the star of everything while leaving the scapegoat entirely out of it. At a school talent show, the CNP will introduce all the parents to one of their children who performed and boast about how talented that child is while not bringing up anything their other child did. This is different than outright telling the child they did a poor job. Instead, they don't acknowledge the scapegoat at all, leaving them to draw their own conclusions and believe they are unworthy of attention.

CNPs also try to brainwash their children. To the CNP, their children's wants and needs do not exist outside of the CNP's desires. Therefore, they won't let their children grow independent. They want to be the source of their children's needs, which stunts their growth and maturation into adulthood. Any activities that the children enjoy, the CNP will try to disturb. They will encourage their children to try things that the CNP likes, but when the children participate in something they enjoy, the CNP devalues it every time. For example, if you want to learn something new that you're passionate about, your CNP parent will find ways to sabotage you. They may repeatedly interrupt your practice sessions or pretend to be helpful while making devastating remarks that destroy your confidence.

Additionally, the CNP will throw crumbs of positive reinforcement to keep you hanging on for more of their approval. Their encouragement is unpredictable, with random moments of praise and respect. The CNP will say that they're proud of you or something else that they know you needed to hear. Unfortunately, they don't mean it the way a loving parent does, as their actions suggest otherwise. They act in this way to both the scapegoat and the golden child. However, the difference is that the golden child typically ends up doing what the CNP wanted them to do in the first place, while the scapegoat child may continue to pursue what they want. After all, the scapegoat's natural independence made them the CNP's target for mistreatment in the first place. If the CNP can't control you, they'll try to hurt you instead.

By undermining their children's self-efficacy, the CNP parent binds their children closer to them. Their children often lack trust in their ability to care for themselves or make their own decisions. This is especially true in the golden child, who may seem like the lucky one to have the parent's affections but isn't overall. The golden child doesn't realize that being the favorite can also be a curse. They're usually the most controlled and trapped within the CNP's web. Unlike the scapegoat who has felt unloved, the golden child, who has been made to feel special, has no reason to separate from the CNP. Thus, they stay with the CNP, who continues to use their emotional abuse tactics on the golden child.

When the healthy parent or the sibling tries to open the eyes of the golden child, they refuse to listen, dutifully blocking out anything negative about the CNP parent. The golden child acts as their parent's flying monkey, defending and praising them. They become isolated from the rest of their family, who see the truth. The CNP's unstable relationships leave an impression on the golden child, preventing them from seeking healthy friendships or partners. They look for people who reflect their CNP parent's qualities because that is who they feel most loved by. After all, the CNP told them that, and why would a parent ever lie to their children?

Deep down, they have never received love or truth from the CNP, which is something kids wish for the most from their parents. Instead, the alienated golden child receives superficial love through materialistic things. They are still being gaslit and unheard, without realizing it. Arguments are left unresolved, and the golden child cannot fully express their opinions. They're worried about being abandoned by the CNP, who instills the idea that they could discard them on a dime. This leaves them emotionally empty inside as they didn't learn the skills to fulfill this void themselves.

The CNP creates a clone of themselves in the golden child by encouraging any immoral behavior. When the child doesn't listen, isn't responsible, or misbehaves, the CNP parent undermines any attempts the healthy parent makes to correct that behavior. When the other parent punishes the golden child for misbehaving, the CNP labels that punishment as emotional abuse. For example, when I took toy or phone privileges away from my children in our marriage, X would make it clear that he disagreed with my parenting at that moment. He never defended me or supported me in any parenting decision. Later, when my older daughter, his golden child, would complain to him, he encouraged it and said that I was being too harsh or abusive. Thus, creating the idea that the child is entitled to act however they would like without having to deal with consequences.

The child then resents the healthy parent and anyone who tries to tell them they're in the wrong. The CNP also brainwashes both children into believing they cannot trust the responsible, good parent. They raise the children with the idea that wrong is right and right is wrong, which leaves a strong impression on the golden child. Such a destructive mentality doesn't allow the child to fit into the norms of society and the laws.

Since the golden child was taught that nothing they do is wrong, they lack the real self-love and strength gained from taking accountability for their actions. When people drift out of their lives, they can't understand why a void is created in them that can't be filled. They try to fill the void with love from the CNP parent, but a CNP has nothing in them to fill it with. The scapegoat was made to feel like nothing from the beginning, so they developed coping mechanisms to protect themselves from the more apparent emotional abuse. Often, how a scapegoat copes is unhealthy and requires therapy to overcome. However, the golden child has not developed coping skills because they didn't think they needed to. The unconscious inner turmoil and void leaves them feeling depressed.

Such feelings of depression often result in mental health disorders such as Dissociative Identity Disorder, Borderline Personality Disorder, Depression, Anxiety, etc. Despite a proper diagnosis of those disorders, the CNP parent still won't believe in it. Therefore, the cycle continues as the mental health and feelings of the child are unacknowledged. Unlike the golden child, the scapegoat will escape the unhealthy family dynamic earlier to enjoy independence. Although they still carry deep scars from being alienated by the narcissistic parent, scapegoats are usually stable enough to recognize their upbringing was unhealthy and to seek therapy or support from outside the family. Unfortunately, the golden child will not be able to do that as quickly. The golden child may never be able to escape the toxicity and can become a CNP themselves.

When a parent hides their abuse and portrays it as love instead, the child has a harder time recognizing the abuse is occurring. CNP parents groom their children for abuse in many different ways. First, they exploit the cultural expectations of parents in society. We are taught from a young age that all parents love and want what is best for their children. When we experience a lack of love and support, we're left sad and confused, blaming the toxic parent for the pain they caused. However, a CNP parent doesn't let their children realize the truth, for all their actions are covert. The goal is to keep their children from discovering that the reason behind all their mental suffering is the CNP parent. This way, they can continue their cycle of abuse. The CNP wants to manipulate their child while concealing evidence of their manipulative tactics.

When my eldest, alienated daughter had to rely on her father for financial means, he used money as a tool to abuse her. He would consistently be late on any payments due, control how much time she could have with her therapist for serious mental health issues, and make it hard for her to choose proper medical professionals because of finances. When she raised these concerns, he would guilt trip her, claiming he lost all his money in the divorce. However, he had no problem spending on extravagant trips, a new car, or other luxury purchases. When she realized that he only seemed to have money troubles regarding her struggles, she began to speak up and express how she felt uncared for as his child.

X reacted by trying to cancel her therapy sessions behind her back and by blame-shifting, calling her spoiled and entitled for wanting the most basic help. Initially, his tactics worked on her, and she felt guilty asking him for money. However, as time went on, with X continuing his tactics of "forgetting" to make payments and being emotionally unavailable as a parent, with educated support from her therapist, my eldest daughter began to realize his behavior was toxic. When she called him out for it, he raged, attempting to utilize all of his manipulative tactics of parental alienation, blame-shifting, guilt-tripping, the whole arsenal. However, this time, she was not fooled by his tactics. When X realized he could no longer conceal the emotional abuse from her, he cut her off financially, and they have barely talked since.

See how easy it is for a CNP to cut off a child financially and emotionally? Once their ploy is exposed and they can no longer use their child as willing supply, the CNP has no use for the child and will discard them. The CNP will use every weapon in their arsenal to keep their child in the dark. However, once their blades become dull to their victim, they simply look for another to abuse without looking back.

## Emotional Incest

Narcissistic parents often become very codependent on their children, especially the golden child. They'll use guilt trips to keep them close, isolate them from developing close bonds with anyone else, and convince them that the other healthy parent is the toxic one. Their desire for constant attention and emotional entrapment turns into *emotional incest.*

With emotional incest, the child is used by the adult for emotional fulfillment. They're forced to support the abusive adult by serving as their sole "trusted confidante." Essentially, they become the narcissist's emotional spouse. Healthy parents do not wish to burden their children with their issues or negative emotions. As parents, we try to shield our children from the bad in the world. Not the covert, narcissistic psychopath. They intend to do the opposite. They bring the child into their problems, confiding in them as they should with a therapist or spouse. This creates stress, anxiety, and depression in the child, who soaks up the negative emotions from their parent like a sponge.

However, emotional incest doesn't stop at oversharing emotionally. In fact, it takes a much darker and more damaging turn. Although there is no direct sexual touch, emotional incestual relationships have a sexualized undertone. The CNP parent expresses graphic interest in the child's physical and sexual development. Unbeknownst to the child, the CNP parent breaks their boundaries through invasions of privacy, sexualized conversation, and gifts. The sexuality is implied rather than physical like the more familiar term, incest. Although there is no direct sexual touch, emotional incestual relationships typically have a sexual undertone that never truly feels right to the child. However, the child cannot and many times refuses to acknowledge it.

My ex would have what he called "talking times" with my eldest daughter, the golden child, in the relationship dynamic between him and our daughters. He would go into her room late at night, past midnight, and they would have over hour-long conversations. I never knew what the conversations were about, but he never had them with my youngest daughter, and my oldest refused to divulge what they talked about.

I often tried to stop the "talking times," but both would push me out, and my daughter would get very upset that I was interrupting their time together. I tried to reason with X that she needed her sleep – he often went in on school nights – but he refused to listen or consider my worries. Later, I learned bits and pieces of their conversations. They typically explored sexual topics, including watching pornography. X would talk to her about his own sexual experiences, creating an unhealthy curiosity in her and a different kind of closeness between them. At the youthful age of twelve, my oldest daughter began to watch porn online. It wasn't your average curious youngster looking up sex online out of wonder. She watched disturbing videos degrading to women and much too kinky for someone her age to view. I had no idea how she got the idea to look that up.

However, once I divorced X and learned more about his insidious behaviors, I now know that he had implanted that curiosity in her young brain. The trauma from the emotional incest has indeed shone through in her relationships. She chooses sexual partners remarkably similar to her father and yet gets neither sexual pleasure nor emotional fulfillment from those relationships. Her relationships end up being short and unmeaningful, leaving her feeling more emotionally reliant on her father, who barely gives her the time of day. She often expresses frustration that her father doesn't want to spend as much time with her anymore, and she suffers from feelings of abandonment. This is because she is so used to her toxic closeness with her father that she doesn't realize she has never had any real connection with him without the emotional incest.

None of this will seem obvious to the child of a CNP. They will take it as the parent showing interest in their growth and maturity. They will also see the CNP as a supportive parent who doesn't shame them for their sexual feelings or desires. What they don't see is the damage the emotional incest creates. While it is important not to shame your child, you must help steer them in a healthy direction. Otherwise, they will have toxic and potentially traumatic sexual experiences.

The CNP never guides the child in the right direction regarding sex. Therefore, a child experiencing emotional incest will gravitate towards what they know in terms of a sexual partner. The people the child expresses interest in are usually similar to their CNP parent. Thus, many victims of emotional incest will continue to attract and be in relationships with abusive partners. Because the child is so used to being abused to the point it's normalized for them, they don't realize that how their partner treats them is also wrong. They can't heal from their past trauma because they relive it with their current lover.

Because the child was forced into an adult role and sexualized early on in life, their natural evolution is stunted without it being blatantly apparent. They believe their needs are secondary to the parent and their future partners. Their purpose is to be an emotional object for another rather than an independent adult. As they mature, the adult victim of emotional incest may experience difficulty in self-care, personality and mood disorders, and the inability to have a healthy sexual and romantic relationship.

However, all hope is not lost. Healing takes time and is possible for victims of emotional incest. Finding a therapist that can read between the lines and identify the occurrence of emotional incest can be highly beneficial. If you aren't sure whether or not your parent is using emotional incest on you, try distancing yourself for however long feels most comfortable. The way they react is a strong indicator of whether emotional incest occurs. A healthy parent recognizes their child's need for space, especially as an adult, and will respect it. However, the CNP parent or emotionally abusive parent will react negatively. They will try to guilt you into spending time with them or force their way through your boundaries. The abusive parent will not allow you to have the space you need and will employ as many manipulative tactics as they need to get you back in their grasp. If a parent must hurt you to get you to spend time with them, they are utilizing emotional incest.

## Parental Alienation

Another form of abuse that occurs, especially with the golden child, is parental alienation. Parental alienation occurs when the toxic parent "alienates" their children from the healthy parent. They fabricate a lie so well that the children see them as the good parent when it is the exact opposite. CNP parents are notorious for alienating their children from the other parent. They aim to deprive their victim of everything that gives the victim purpose and happiness. In many cases, the source of the healthy parent's joy is raising their children. Therefore, the CNP becomes perpetually determined to tear that away from their victim at their own children's expense.

It is often successful when one or more children identify stronger with one parent. Throughout the life of those children, the CNP parent has set the groundwork for parental alienation. While both parents are still together, alienation is developed over the years. The CNP parent will start with subtle digs about how the parenting style of the other is harmful or abusive. They capitalize on times when the children have gotten disciplined, empathizing with them rather than supporting the other parent's decision. If a child loses privileges for misbehaving, the CNP makes sure to assert their opinion that the punishment occurring, however minor, is abuse. For example, suppose you decided to take your child's phone privileges away for the day because they didn't finish their homework on time. In that case, the CNP parent will blatantly disagree with that decision, arguing with you about it in front of the child. They aim to ensure the child sees that they are taking the child's side. Later, they'll tell the child how they feel the punishment was too strict. They may try to sneak the phone back to the child.

The CNP parent wants to make sure they are the favorite and more fun parent. This way, when they separate from their spouse, the child follows suit and separates from the healthy parent. The other parent is hated and discarded by the children without a justifiable reason. As the parents separate, the CNP parent pressures their child to hate the other parent just as they do. They'll smear campaign the other parent to the child, criticize everything they do, and try to interfere with their relationship. Both alienated parent and child suffer consequently. The loss of the child and the other parent is comparable to actual death; the grieving process is quite similar. The child harbors feelings of strong resentment, anger, and neglect, which can lead to emotional disorders, disassociation, codependence on the CNP parent, etc. No good comes out of alienating a child from their healthy parent.

No parent is perfect, and all have their bad days. However, an alienated child will not see it that way and severely criticizes the parent for any negative behavior, regardless of an apology or efforts to make it up to the child. The child refuses to hear the other parent's side of the story, listening only to the CNP parent's version of the events. They also block out any good memories with the healthy parent, having been trained to remember the bad. Yet, the CNP parent can do no wrong. They will defend their chosen parent, thinking everything you do is wrong. If the CNP Parent does something wrong, they justify it with whatever sob story the CNP gives them, and the child firmly believes the behavior is acceptable because of it.

The alienated child will have no idea they are influenced by the CNP parent, insisting that their opinions are their own. They feel no remorse for hurting the alienated parent because they feel justified by the story spun by the CNP parent about the healthy parent. To cope with the alienation, children will suppress any good memories with the targeted parent and claim they never enjoyed their time together, despite there being little evidence to support that belief.

When a child has no valid reason to reject a parent and is vehemently against having any contact with them or their extended parent, it is apparent that parental alienation has occurred. Some alienated children have no idea why they specifically hate the targeted parent. Rather, they mirror the thoughts and feelings of the alienating parent. To the healthy parent, their reasoning for wanting to have No Contact with them seems completely ridiculous. However, to the child, it is perfectly reasonable.

In fact, the alienator does something called, *Imprinting*, or rewriting history, which is when they corrupt their kids with false memories, mainly of the healthy parent. If a child recalls a negative memory, especially one caused by the alienator, the CNP parent will turn it around on the other parent, claiming they are the one that caused the painful memory to occur. For example, suppose the narcissist thought of an idea for punishment or agreed to a punishment for a child's unruly behavior. The CNP will tell the child it was all the healthy parent's idea and that they tried to stop the punishment from occurring. This way, the anger is not directed toward the CNP but the healthy parent instead.

The child's hostility toward the targeted parent can also be directed toward the parent's extended family. My alienated child is a direct example of this behavior. X alienated her throughout our married life but especially sunk his claws into her when we separated.

She refused to hear my side of the story, solely believing I was the reason we were getting divorced. Though X acted in unspeakable ways throughout the divorce, she supported his actions, although they were so obviously abusive. Instead, without fail, it became my fault.

I gave her the space she needed and mourned the loss of our relationship. I had no idea her resentment towards me would gravitate towards the rest of her family. Her grandparents, who expressed love and care towards her as a child, were suddenly toxic to her. Though they were growing older, she refused to speak to them, convinced they had some insidious goal to get her back in my grasp. In truth, they missed her and wanted to hear how her life was going. Before my mother passed away, she hoped my alienated child would call her, but she never did. When she passed away, my youngest daughter mentioned that my alienated child had no mournful words to say other than that she felt like she never really knew her.

This was because X had made it seem like they were conspiring against her, contrasting with how they treated her when she was young. Therefore, she couldn't know her grandparents when X's negativity distorted her happy memories. It was a devastating situation for everyone involved, except, of course, X.

Though the golden child is often looked at as the "lucky" one, they are as much a victim of abuse from the narcissistic parent as the scapegoat is. In healthy parent-child relationships, the idea of choosing favorites is abominable. Parents are responsible for giving their children a happy upbringing and shielding them from trauma rather than giving it to them. Therefore, a child whose parent has scapegoated them does not have that parent. The golden child, who may choose to live with the narcissistic parent, doesn't have the emotional support and genuine love a child needs from their parent. Biologically, the narcissist is their parent, but they are not a real parent in the ways that count.

### Types of toxic parent-child relationships that also occur:

- The absent parent chooses not to take any responsibility for raising their child or engaging in their life.
- Constantly disrespects or abuses spouse (in father-daughter relationships, it becomes likely the daughter will be attracted to men who treat her the same way).
- Goes out of their way to dismiss or invalidate their child's feelings.
- Wants to be the best at everything they do and consider parenting a competition.
- Uses fear and punishment to keep the child's behavior in control.
- Doesn't show much interest in their child's life and fails to provide support or comfort when needed.
- They hold constant, high standards for their kid and complain about the child's behavior, belittling their achievements.

- Doesn't provide a sense of safety.
- Emotionally, physically, or sexually abusive parents.

The biggest takeaway I want you to have from this chapter is to pay attention to actions and not words. Although we want to see the best in our parents and have that parental love, sometimes a parent is just toxic. Often, the people we want to trust instinctively are the ones that let us down the most. The best thing you can do is evaluate how your parent or guardian makes you feel daily and whether you truly feel supported, loved, and cared for. Words are not enough. It is the actions of an individual that proves whether they are healthy and worthy of your trust.

# Chapter 7: Divorcing a Covert, Narcissistic Psychopath

Divorcing a CNP is no simple process. The truths one discovers about their partner are unthinkable and life-changing, but not in a good way. The best way I can begin to explain how horrifically unique it is to divorce a CNP is to tell you my story.

It is most important to note that divorcing a CNP or simply a Covert Narcissist is quite different from divorcing an Overt Narcissist. The only word that comes to mind to describe it is sneaky. Sneaky in that they prepare for the divorce years in advance, including at the beginning of the marriage. My ex-husband financially prepared himself for the divorce for years before we married by not fully disclosing all his assets before marriage, hiding assets and money separate from the community property, and keeping spreadsheets and tabs of everything spent on our children, home, and living needs to be paid back to him in the event of divorce.

I had access to one joint account, which he controlled and which I trustingly put any earnings into as he claimed it was necessary for the financial welfare of the children and their education. He planned and left a visible trace of the bare minimum of our marital wealth, which would later be used to pay the legal fees. He worked around state laws to keep the money hidden, storing it in a different country and within his side of the family. He also hid under the name of our eldest, his golden child's name, knowing she'd have no interest or desire to learn anything about it.

Then, during the divorce, he gained most of the finances, leaving me little to move on. He drew the divorce out longer than usual, almost three years, to drain me of what little money I had and to continue to get narcissistic supply. When something was required of him, he either put it off too long or didn't do it at all, resulting in multiple court violations, for which he was not reprimanded. Though he claimed to want the split to be amicable, his covert tactics ensured that he ended up the winning party. No one wins with CNPs. Everyone loses more than ever should in a lifetime.

Though the divorce was a terrible period of my life, I am still glad I made it out and am now living without my CNP ex's influence. We were together for twenty-seven years, twenty-four married, and all used and abused. I was chronically ill, financially controlled, and physically and psychologically abused by X. My strong faith and belief in old-fashioned morals of not wanting to be divorced kept me prisoner to the toxic relationship. I missed the red flags at the beginning of our relationship. I didn't know they existed or that red flags were something to look for! I was young and naïve, and he had a full nine years of age on me. He knew what he was doing and wore his mask well. I didn't come from a broken home like his. I'd die for my family and the hope that my kids could have a loving home.

However, there is a breaking point. When I realized our home life was already dysfunctional and how it negatively impacted the children, I knew it was time to get out. Still, I felt stuck. I didn't know how to escape as he controlled everything from the money down to the schedule. But X was already prepared for the discard phase.

During Thanksgiving, while he stayed with our children at my family home with my parents, he cowardly sent me an email saying we should move on. After his email, I asked X if he was another person, to which he replied by gaslighting and claiming he still loved me, but our marriage had been over since the seventh year of it. I guess I missed the memo because we'd just had our first kid together at that time.

X claimed no fault and didn't state the word divorce in the email. The tone was confusing, suggesting we split without directly saying the words—another way to gaslight me.

I felt blindsided. Though I knew we weren't in a happy place, I thought that it would change. That X could change. I wanted the man I thought I knew before we got married, the man I had fallen in love with. I hadn't seen that man for twenty-four years, but I had clung to the hope that he would return. That once he was retired and work could no longer be an excuse, he would again be committed to his family. My hope had been misguided. I had begun to stop reacting to his abusive tactics, simply walking away and shutting the door instead of engaging in a fight with him. He was ready to discard me, unable to get any more narcissistic supply. Since he had no reason to wear his mask, he began to let it slip more to unsettle me further.

During their Thanksgiving visit to my parent's home with our daughters (I was too ill to travel), he removed a photo of me from the wall of their home, greatly upsetting my mother. When she confronted him about it, he said he hadn't thought of his actions, only that he couldn't stand to look at me. After all, I was a reminder of everything he wasn't, empathetic, truthful, and faithful. My mother was mortified at first but not surprised. She had a good judge of character, telling me the first time she met him that I shouldn't be with him. Moments before my marriage, she tried to open my eyes, but my heart had been fooled by the love-bombing stage, my lack of dating experience, and my youth. This is a common tactic of predators like him, seeking out much younger supplies with less life experience so they can easily manipulate and control them.

After these blindsides, I knew in my gut that our marriage had been a sham. Yet, I was to find more proof of how secretive X was. You know the saying, "a little bird told me?" In my case, it was a little bat. After Thanksgiving, upon their return, I asked if X could bring the garbage bins up from the street. He never helped around the house on his merit, for he felt he was above that. After much complaining, he finally agreed to do it. From the window, I saw him suddenly start jumping up and down. X ran back home and said a bat had just attacked him.

He pointed out a tiny hole in his shirt and yelled, "get the f'ing garbage bins yourself. I'm not going out there to be attacked again." How chivalrous.

The next day, my youngest daughter got a rare glimpse of his phone in which a text popped up saying, "Oh no, that was my favorite shirt on you!" from another woman, whom he claimed was his coworker.

She didn't believe her father was a cheater, but something about that text seemed too intimate for a coworker. My youngest got her full name, and I looked it up, finding out that she lived precisely where X had been going on "business trips" for many years. We also recalled how he had mentioned her name in the past, bragging about how he'd met a new woman in the same industry as him. Not being a jealous person, I had thought it was nice he was supportive of women in his industry. Yet another red flag I'd missed.

Once I'd heard about the texts and looked up the woman online, I decided to check the credit card statements to find more proof. Sure enough, there was a charge for two tickets to the Singapore zoo, where he was supposed to be on a business trip. X never cared for the zoo, nor animals in general. It wasn't as if he was going with a group of work buddies. Instead, he purchased a ticket for someone else. It was at that point that I decided to confront him.

Without hesitation, I asked, "how was your date at the Singapore zoo?"

At first, he was shocked and tried to deny it, but I'd had enough. I looked him dead in the eyes and told him to stop being a coward and own up to it. A narcissist takes ultimate offense to being called a coward. When he looked at me, his eyes were cold, empty, harsh, and eerie. I felt like I was staring straight into the eyes of the devil himself. An overwhelming calm washed over me, and I knew not to push him any further, or it could be dangerous to my life. My youngest hid behind the garage door listening in as she'd needed proof of the feelings I've felt and expressed several times throughout the years.

Indeed, he finally admitted that he was with her and that they felt they would have a happy life together. At that very moment, he crossed the one line that was it for me. We openly discussed that we'd never cheat on one another, and if we fell out of love or found new love, we'd let the other know before doing the lowest form of betrayal, cheating. I knew there was no saving this marriage, for there was never any real marriage. It was all an act. Fraud. A one-sided lie.

I endured years of torrential hell and the most degrading treatment anyone could endure. It had felt like a slow death and an erasing of my existence as a wife and a mother. He'd moved on to another person for new narcissistic supply as mine had officially reached its limit. He knew I could now see through his lies and deception. I'd thought his mask was at last removed, but what he'd done to our family, to one of our daughters, would soon come to light.

I wanted answers. I wanted to know how this blindside had occurred. *Why* it had occurred. After midnight, X agreed to have a family meeting to discuss all that had happened. All that he'd done. I was tired from a long day, but we wanted answers. Needed answers. Deserved answers. But what I got instead was more confusion, more word salad, gaslighting, blame-shifting, projection, and triangulation. X had somehow convinced our oldest daughter into taking the blame for him deciding to end our marriage. She admitted to telling him we should separate, and he did not disagree. Now there was no blood on his hands, so he thought. He let our eldest daughter adopt the blame, not bothering to take any accountability himself. Our marriage hadn't been joyful, and my eldest said no one should be so unhappy. Granted, she was right, but her following words were borderline disturbing.

She suggested I try to hook up with the husband of X's girlfriend, who didn't know he was being cheated on! I was mortified to hear such words coming from her mouth and more distraught to realize that my daughter had become one of his flying monkeys, willing to cause hurt and pain without any regard for my feelings as a human being and her parent.

After that night, I'd had enough. There was no saving our marriage. Already, a trickle of resentment towards me ran deep within our oldest daughter, like poison settling in every crevice of her mind. I could not let this go on any longer, but it was difficult to know where to begin. X had already begun discussing plans with a divorce lawyer months before sending the email. He was two steps ahead before I made one step. I combed the internet for lawyers, read every good and negative review, and learned how costly the process would be. Not only had I been a stay-at-home mom during our marriage, but I was also chronically ill. I had no consistent income, and any money I did have, I'd put into our joint account. Still, I had no other option. I found a lawyer and put the retainer fee on our joint credit card. Though my funds weren't much, I had contributed financially, faithfully, physically, and emotionally to our marriage.

My lawyer advised me to serve him quickly, stating it is better to serve than get served. Nothing was more satisfying at that time than seeing the utter disbelief on his face when he got served. Although it felt good to be a step ahead, I still hid behind the stairs, worried that his reaction could get physically violent. The door he slammed – which, in the past, he slammed to the point of breaking - and the several items he threw around his office in his fit of rage surely suffered. Though he had spoken with attorneys, he had not hired one yet.

The night before, X had tried to hoover me back by sending a text asking if we should still give this marriage another try. It was the first text of his I never answered and one that deserved no answer. No more tries were left in our marriage, though, not with another woman in the picture. Another woman he had dated, traveled with, spent our community earnings on, and slept with for years behind my back. I would not consider one more minute with this creature as he no longer was a man in my mind. I had to refocus. It was time to save myself and our children. But my troubles did not end with the start of the divorce. Unfortunately, they grew vaster and far more intoxicating.

It is one thing to be married to a covert, narcissistic psychopath. It is another to divorce one. Narcissists are secretive during marriage but are more underhanded during the divorce. The worst part is, they get away with it! We had several backup computer servers in the home, all password protected by X, to which I had limited access. Just a few days into the divorce, the servers were suddenly gone. When I asked him about it, he said he would not return them because I had blocked access to one of the servers.

Before that exchange, I had locked the door to where this server was stored because he hid it in the closet under the stairs where our Wi-Fi, Routers, security cameras, and Cable TV were located. He kept causing stress by turning off the Wi-Fi, security cameras, and TV. He denied doing so, leaving me confused and gaslit until I caught him one night. I had gone downstairs quietly so as not to disturb my daughter's sleep, and as I made my way to the room, I noticed him sneaking out quietly, just as the tv went blank again. It seemed to go blank when I went to bed as he knew I needed it to fall asleep. I suspected he was tampering with it because prior to the divorce, it worked just fine. When he was gone on all his trips, it worked fine. All of a sudden, the TV and Wi-Fi had stopped working like clockwork in the late evenings to the point my daughter couldn't get her homework done due to having no internet connection.

He was unplugging cables in what I called the tech closet. After he left and snuck back into his office, I went in and saw several cables dangling. When I plugged the cables he'd pulled out back in, the TV, cameras, and Wi-Fi suddenly started to work again. He had been gaslighting me for the longest time, saying the connectivity was probably failing or the speed rate was low. All sorts of concocted lies to frustrate and cause me stress. There was so much during the marriage that it was nothing new to me, and I no longer reacted.

Instead, I took action. X left for yet another trip which gave me the perfect opportunity to hire a locksmith to swap out the doorknobs for ones that required a key that only I had access to. I had him do my bedroom and office as I felt unsafe in my home. X never let me know when he was leaving nor coming and would trigger the house alarm in the early hours of the night, startling both myself and our daughter countless times. I tried to reason with him to stop causing us such fear and stress, and he looked me dead in the face with that narcissistic smirk and just laughed.

When X refused to bring back the servers he had stolen from our home, I had to call the police for help. It was community property with years of joint finances, photos, videos, taxes, receipts, and more. I knew he was wiping them, or at least what he was hiding on them, clean. X told the officers exactly what he was doing; he said *I* was the one erasing the other server X hid in the tech closet, so he had to protect them by moving them out. I didn't know how to work the servers, let alone erase them, but the police officers believed him. It had turned out that there was one more server hidden in the tech room that X had not taken out yet but had desperately wanted to get access to for a reason I never found out. When he brought the other servers back, they were wiped clean with the passwords changed.

After this situation, my divorce team told me to check my computer for spyware. I didn't believe there could be anything on my computer. I was still naïve. They had been right. My and our adult kids' computers had a spyware and cloud backup app called CrashPlan. All our texts, emails to friends, family, lawyers, and more were being stored and accessed by him. I was advised to shut my computer down immediately and buy a new one. Although what he did was illegal, he was never held accountable for his actions in court.

In a divorce, Discovery occurs when you provide the attorneys with the history and financial documents to divide community assets equally between the two parties. However, with a CNP, an equal split is not possible. X set up a Dropbox for the legal teams filled with thousands of useless files to cause confusion and drag the case out further. This is a tactic used by opposing parties in many areas of law.

The opposing party can waste the other party's time and money by sending thousands of documents rather than just the ones requested. A weaker legal team may be unable to find the document needed, or it could be disregarded altogether. The entire strategy is meant to gaslight, confuse, and distract.

In my divorce, I had to file costly subpoenas to an insane amount of financial accounts that X had failed to provide promptly. He had canceled the one joint card we had and emptied our joint account, hiding all the funds under his name, his family members' names, and in other countries. Since I didn't have access to any of the documents, I had to resort to digging through his office while he traveled. I was shocked to find hidden cash in many places and scanned the documents I could find. Still, no one deigned to look at the documents I'd found, believing his word above factual proof. Being the less financially secure party in the divorce left me with no voice, no parity, and no ability to pay for any justice. I had to pay for costly hearings to get community funds just to pay for legal fees, which created a vicious, endless cycle of financial abuse.

Both X's and my lawyer were greedy, protecting the CNP to get rich off of him. My first lawyer mixed up my case with another's and didn't catch X buying a second home illegally with community funds, which is an ATROS Violation (which he committed many and was never penalized for). ATROS stands for Automatic Restraining Orders and specifies what divorced parties can and cannot do with the community funds. For example, you may use community funds to obtain a lawyer and pay for legal fees but using it to buy a home without notifying one's spouse and the court is a violation. Still, little weight tends to be put on ATROS violations, so a more manipulative or wealthier person can get away with it if your legal team does not spot it in enough time. That happened many times, and X continued transferring our funds into new accounts to create a well-executed tracing nightmare.

Having a strong and experienced lawyer is critical when divorcing a CNP. The CNP, especially if they hold the majority of the funds, will not hold back with their legal team, often hiring lawyers who want to win at all costs or drain the community funds with their fees. In my case, I did not have the good fortune of having a powerful legal team and suffered greatly for it. With my second attorney, seconds before our case appeared in front of the court-ordered judge, the teams began deal-making. Unbeknownst to me, the attorneys signed a stipulation on a low spousal support number of X's choosing and changed the agreed-upon start date to a month later, something my lawyer missed under time pressure as our case was coming up before the judge. For another month, I had no support for my child and me to live on and no way to pay legal fees. My case never made it in front of that judge again, for they moved our case to an old, retired, private judge, whom I was advised under extreme duress to agree upon hiring to keep the case moving.

After the fiasco of X buying a home behind my back, it began to get worse from there. His mask was off, showing his not-so-new but more dangerous side. When it was finally time for him to move out, I had decided to go "No-Contact" with him and relied on the attorney. We had previously tried to write a list of what belongings we both wanted to keep. Still, it became another endless, costly, gaslighting tactic as he kept making changes to the list, suddenly wanting things previously agreed on that I had requested, though he had shown no interest in them before. After such trouble from just a simple task and over 15 spreadsheets later, I knew nothing would be amicably resolved from there on out. From learning of his thievery from community funds, there was no trust left to be had.

X was traveling again, and the day he returned, he mentioned he had a moving truck coming in the morning to collect his things. There was no discussion with me, the lawyers, no one. In X's mind, everything was his. The thing with CNPs is they genuinely believe in their mind they own you and anything associated with you. Another blindside! I had no money, and now I would be left with no means to purchase things for my daughter and my new place that I had yet to find. X had been pushing the private judge to force my daughter and me out of our home.

I had less than 24 hours to safeguard what belonged to us that he had no care for but would take to cause further duress and suffering. He left for lunch, and I immediately contacted the locksmith I had hired in the past, begging for an emergency re-key of our home locks. There were several doors to do. He said he was on his way, and I couldn't believe he'd drop everything to help me like this. Little did I know he'd become my savior and witness to X's rage.

I'm forever grateful to that locksmith and believe he saved my life. He worked quickly and tirelessly, locking every door behind him as he worked and finished before X arrived home. He asked me if it would be safe for him to leave, a question I wasn't sure I had the answer to. However, X provided the answer to his query rather quickly. As you may recall from Chapter 5, when he arrived, he was furious and demanded a set of keys from the locksmith, chasing me around the house until I begged the locksmith for help. As you may remember from Chapter 5, when the police arrived, they took his side, convinced I was the dangerous one instead.

The officers instructed my attorney that X had the right to gather a few of his belongings, clothes, and work laptop. My attorney instructed them that he was to take nothing more as he previously stole community property, and none of it was divided yet in the divorce. Everything was to remain in the community property home until assets were legally split. The officers were sympathetic to X and treated me like a felon. They followed him through the house to retrieve a few items before making him leave. I asked the two officers if they would call and speak to the locksmith and at least hear my side of the story.

I couldn't believe I had been silenced while only X was heard. I still had absolutely no voice. I begged them to please listen to my side. They refused.

"It's because of police officers like you that we remain battered, our lives taken from abusers such as X," I stated bluntly.

One of the officers apologized and expressed remorse, belief, and empathy for what I was going through. The other could care less. This is the reason I would never reach out to the police for help again. They weren't there to serve and protect those who deserved and needed it.

I've learned you are on your own in this world. The law is not on your side. The law is on the side of the ones that pay them.

I've also come to be humbled by strangers in my community helping me as I fell on tough times. I had to let go of my pride and fears to ask for help. I remember my neighbor asked why the police had come. When I explained the situation to her, she was appalled. She tucked a hundred dollars into the palm of my daughter's hand when she learned we had no support yet due to the underhandedness of the lawyers. I remember her words so clearly. She said to my daughter don't buy anything boring. Buy something that brings a smile to your face. Use it for fun. I was in tears.

We used it for gas for her car so she could get to school and food for her lunches at school. I reached out to old friends I hadn't spoken to in a while, and it was as if we had never lost touch. Those who were busy stopped to spend time comforting and helping me. I was finally finding my way back to those who cared about me and vice versa. I felt safe, not as alone as I had felt throughout my marriage and relationship.

When the moving truck came the next day, my eldest daughter moved out with him. She was brainwashed. She became his flying monkey, refusing to hear my side in the divorce. I tried to reach out to her to let her know that I loved her and would never intentionally harm her, but it was too late. On moving day, she instigated immature behavior, not following the court orders and trying to take belongings that were not hers. She danced mockingly in front of the home cameras, and her actions were brought to my attention by the security guard watching the ordeal. It was a sad day to see the daughter I had loved, provided for, and tried to raise as best I could reduce herself to childish and hateful behavior. X and my daughter ended up calling the police as he wanted more items not on the legal division of assets list. When I presented the court order to the police with my lawyer on the phone, he saw that X's list was a fake and told him to finish and leave. That was about one of the sole times there was any sort of legal justice in my case.

It got more complicated with the home sale. I had hired a real estate agent who reached out to me through social media, emphasizing with my situation and claiming she wanted to help. As I talked about in Chapter 2, she turned out to be meddlesome and just as toxic as X. The situation revealed a CNP's manipulative power over others outside the family. Someone who had claimed to be on my side or at the very least impartial ended up taking the CNP's side and discarding the code of ethics they claim to be bound by.

Though the drama of the home sale was traumatic in itself, with all the gaslighting and negativity, it was almost nothing compared to the utter frustration that was dealing with the unjust legal system. If you haven't been in the legal world, you believe that truth and morality will prevail. But family law is a damaged system, one that benefits the wealthy and harms the less fortunate. It's great for the lawyers who bank off dysfunctional and abusive situations, but in the end, the children often pay for the disagreements between parents. If I could say one thing I was grateful for about my divorce is that my children were adults, and we did not have to go through an awful custody battle.

As I discussed earlier, one of the greatest mistakes I did make in the divorce was agreeing to hire a private judge. The attorneys recommended one, saying it would help the case move faster and be less costly. This is an absolute falsity in my experience, and I encourage any reader facing divorce or considering not to hire a private judge. You may end up with a better judge appointed by the court than one chosen by the attorneys who all have their own connections beyond the scope of your knowledge. Once you hire a private judge, it becomes too late to change your mind and becomes a significant financial sink. The judge we hired banked $650 an hour, texted on her phone during hearings, and didn't read a single document nor remember the case between hearings. The hearings mostly took place on the phone while she ate or took her personal phone call breaks. Her title allowed her to rule based on her mood of the day, not by impartial law-following. Truth and visible facts weren't accepted into evidence.

At this point, I had already hired three lawyers, the first two I had to fire due to their negligence in my case. When you cannot afford the legal fees of a strong, well-known lawyer, it is not unusual to have to go through several different attorneys throughout a long, drawn-out case. As you may recall, one of the lawyers missed X's purchase of a home with community funds. I told the second lawyer that the prenup X offered as evidence had never been signed by me and was altered and embellished. The signature on it was X's handwriting and utter forgery. However, unbeknownst to me, the lawyer sanctioned an agreement stating I had indeed signed the prenup, which ultimately ruined the rest of my case. Towards the end, he became aggressive and verbally abusive to the point I knew I couldn't work with him anymore.

Between firing my second lawyer and hiring my last one, I had to represent myself against X and his legal team. X's lawyer took advantage of this, racking up the hours by sending bogus letters and overwhelming me with threatening emails. I tried to put it behind me, focusing on submitting my factual evidence and hoping for some kind of parity. The experience was disturbing in itself. The judge didn't allow me to speak one word and solely listened to X's attorney during our phone hearing. My second attorney admitted fault in his deposition, but the testimony was ignored.

In my deposition by X's attorney, they asked me which lawyers I interviewed, and I listed them out, with X's new attorney being one of them. Legally, he had an obligation not to take X as a client as he heard of our case from me first, which was a conflict of interest. Well, it turned out that this new attorney and the Judge were friends and went to the same religious ceremonies together. So again, heed my warnings, do not hire a private Judge under any circumstance.

My third and final lawyer was the worst, but at this point, after two years of this burden, I was done. My last lawyer was more concerned about her image and fitting in with the "big boys" on X's side than being dedicated to my case. The judge and X's lawyer scoffed at her during hearings. She was only more of a financial burden to my case.

At that point, I knew there was no way I would ever get parity, a voice, or justice. It wasn't worth investing a cent more into a losing battle. I was in a dark place, feeling trapped in a pit of hopelessness. But a light shone into my pit of despair, and that was my father. My daughter and I are blessed to have him as our role model for what a real man, father, and grandfather are. His example is why I was easily fooled by X, for I had seen what a good marriage and loving husband were. I had no idea such a thing as red flags existed or that a person could be so unbelievably cruel with utter hatred to their spouse and mother of their children. I am grateful my child will know what to look for but sad about what we had to endure to learn about toxic relationships.

My father saw the legal abuse and frauds for what and who they were. He took the time to negotiate with X to free me from it all as he couldn't watch me endure it anymore. I don't regret fighting for my rights and justice as I showed myself and my daughter self-worth, self-care, and pushing through when all the odds are stacked against you. I wanted to be able to keep providing for my child, her college, future, and dreams. In the end, we reached a more beneficial settlement to X, but that allowed me to escape domestic, financial, and legal abuse for good.

He kept our hidden marital wealth that we grew together while still crying to our daughters that I robbed him of his retirement. He makes well over a million alone in his paycheck yearly and has so much wealth from our investments that his entire family and our kids could live comfortable lives. He managed to own three homes during our divorce, yet he cried poor to the Judge, lawyers, and our kids. He'd not give a dime towards our daughter's college education and encouraged her to go into financial aid debt rather than help her achieve her dreams. And, in his deluded mind, he believes himself to be a terrific father. CNPs wholly believe their lies and will take you down the rabbit hole with them into darkness. There is no light at the end of the tunnel with a covert, narcissistic psychopath.

Now that you know my story, I want to share with you all that I have learned so that you, dear reader, may not suffer as I did whether you are considering, have already filed for, or are in the midst of a divorce. If you are not thinking in that direction, it is still important to be knowledgeable about such legal matters, and knowing the facts does no harm. Many are hesitant to educate themselves as it is considered a jinx to a happy marriage or a lack of trust in one's partner. However, I do not see it that way after what I went through.

After all, you don't avoid the ocean altogether to evade harm; you educate yourself on the high tides and ocean life activity in your area to maintain the appropriate caution to protect yourself. No damage comes from arming yourself with knowledge, and those that disagree could be the real problem. A healthy spouse would want you to know how to protect yourself from the narcissists of this world, as there are far too many.

There is so much I wish I had known amidst my divorce. For one thing, I wish I'd known the word narcissist and what it truly meant. I only knew the surface definition of the word, not that it was an actual personality disorder. Had I been aware of narcissism, there are many things I would have done differently in my marriage and divorce. I wish there had been a book like this to guide me through my divorce.

As you've learned, a divorce with a CNP is unlike any other. They change everything just and righteous about the divorce system to best fit their needs. People and attorneys alike tend to move towards settlement. However, a narcissist prefers going to court and having the judge decide because they don't have to take responsibility for the outcome, especially if it is not in their favor. Whether they win or lose, it is not the narcissist's fault. This allows them to maintain at least the illusion of control in the end.

A CNPs main goal is to extend the divorce for as long as possible. It is common for a narcissist to file lots of motions, request more time, have delays, and fabricate emergencies. No matter what, the narcissist plays the victim, retelling the marriage and divorce proceedings in a way that favors them. They have no qualms with lying in sworn documents, regardless of their provability, as long as it takes up more time, paperwork, and legal fees. Other ways they extend the length of the divorce include not showing up for court dates, including misleading information in filings and appeals that need to be challenged, and not disclosing information, so more discovery is needed. Though they use all these tactics, the CNP will blame the other party for all of these inconveniences. This way, they appear all the more believable to the judge.

Prepare to be smear-campaigned by the narcissist to friends, family, and anyone who will listen. With CNPs, it is more dangerous, for they are very covert about it. They will act as though they aren't willing to give information about you freely, instead having people pull it out of them when that was their intention all along. This makes them appear more credible rather than voluntarily spewing negativity about you wherever they go. Instead, they carefully manipulate others against you, placing hints of malice within their subconscious and allowing it to grow.

CNPs also refuse to negotiate or settle. They make lowball settlement offers and fail to respond to any other matters presented. Unfortunately, there is no middle ground with narcissists as they will continue to insist on their position, regardless of any new facts or information presented. Once you eventually come to a settlement, some CNPs will try to keep bringing you back to court.

When children are involved, the conflict can be endless. Different ways a CNP can keep weaving their tapestry of abuse include:

- Lack of communication when managing time with the children
- Having to share schedules for appointments or activities
- Challenges with picking children up from school and legal appointed time
- Not paying bills or child support on time
- Interfering in the privacy of a child,
- Sending frequent emails of a harassing nature
- Parental alienation
- The constant grilling of the child about the parent

These issues become ones that must be, once again, resolved in court.

Here are the pointers you need to know when divorcing a covert, narcissistic psychopath to liberate yourself from their clutches faster.

## Hide Your Cards

This is the first and most important tip: never tell your soon-to-be-ex, especially a CNP, anything. Withhold all details of your case and your life. CNPs will use any tidbit of information they can get against you, no matter how small. Reveal your cards to a CNP and risk them using what you give to their advantage.

CNPs are particularly crafty when it comes to getting information out of people. They usually start conversational, asking you about your day or keeping the talk light-hearted. Then, when your guard is down, they will ask deeper questions so that you don't notice how much information you're giving away. It may seem like another simple question until you realize you said too much.

The CNP will also accuse you of lying or give you a doubtful look so that you feel the need to explain yourself more to prove your innocence. But you must remember, there is no need for you to have to explain yourself to anyone, not just the CNP. Whether or not they choose to believe you is on them. Less is more when speaking to a CNP and hiding your cards will serve you well in the long run.

## Ensure Your Safety

Divorces with a narcissist become very ugly, and narcissists become more abusive and dangerous as their anger grows. Make sure you have security cameras, let safe family members know about your situation and location, or trust a close friend who does not know the CNP with your whereabouts if you must contact the CNP. If you're in immediate danger and your ex shows violent tendencies, find another place to live without letting the CNP know where you are.

Under no circumstances, no matter how much the CNP promises they will change, should you reveal your location to the CNP. They will never change and only use love-bombing tactics to hoover you back into their control.

On the other hand, if it is safe enough to stay in the house, don't leave it, or the CNP will sell it behind your back. However, your safety is of the utmost importance. If you ever feel like you are in a dangerous situation, remove yourself as soon as possible.

## Save Your Own Money

This tip applies to all relationships. Many people think it is a lack of trust or foreshadowing of a marriage ending if they keep money separately rather than in a joint account. While the idea of sharing money is a lovely ideal, it is not realistic, especially in this century. It is better to have a backup plan than no plan at all. Ensure that you have a way to make your own money and save it at all times. Life can change in so many unfathomable ways that it is imperative you financially protect yourself. I put most of the money I earned into our joint accounts throughout my marriage with X, only to be left with barely anything to live off of when we divorced.

Keep a bank account for yourself that your spouse doesn't have access to. Don't let one partner solely handle all the finances. And, if you are a stay-at-home parent, make sure to put money aside for yourself. This is not about going into a marriage with a mindset of failing but about being financially independent and protecting yourself.

Remember, marriage is a *partnership*. The money should never be controlled or managed by one side.

## Don't Discuss Divorce

When you're in the middle of a divorce, never discuss it with your ex. Keep it between you and your lawyer, no matter how agreeable they may seem. Any information you give them about your case, your plans, your lawyer, etc., can be used against you by the other side. If your soon-to-be-ex asks questions regarding your separation, simply respond with, "I am not at liberty to discuss this information." They do not need to know what is going on with your side.

After all, you're separating for a reason. Sharing information won't make your ex go easy on you in hearings, nor will it make them sympathetic to your side. Remember, as a CNP, they don't possess empathy or emotional intelligence. They are robotic, broken machines.

## Do the Detective Work

If you share or shared any devices with your soon-to-be-ex, make sure they have no access to them anymore – that is, if you own the device. If you don't own it, make sure to wipe the device clean of your information – and check for spyware. Search the applications for any app that seems suspicious, or you don't remember downloading. Sometimes these apps have other software uses to act as a decoy. If you don't recognize something, research it. Change any passwords you may have shared. I found out, during my divorce, X kept a spreadsheet of all my and our children's passwords.

Check your home for hidden cameras or microphones. This may seem like something out of a movie, but it does happen! Not only is it illegal, but it is a severe breach of privacy and could give your soon-to-be-ex an edge in the divorce.

Lastly, make sure you download and save any information you have access to before the divorce begins without the CNP knowing. Try to discover their hidden accounts, as most CNPs have accounts hidden from you. Anything they don't store on a computer will be hidden in their private room, office, safes, etc. Try to search it all as best as you can. It is eerie to learn how much your spouse has hidden from you, but it is better to know it all rather than stay in the dark. Make sure to save copies of anything you find, especially if it relates to the divorce.

## Interview, Interview, Interview

Interview as many lawyers as you can. There's a trick you can use to get yourself on even ground with a wealthier spouse and especially one who is a narcissist. Many attorneys ask for a consultation fee, but the expense of that fee can be worth it, for the more you interview, the more lawyers know your case. Therefore, they most likely will not be able to represent your ex as it would be a conflict of interest. Try to hit up all the top lawyers in your city or county. This way, if you can't afford the best lawyer, your ex won't be able to hire them either. This evens the playing field just a bit between spouses. As it was in my case, some lawyers have no ethics nor scruples, so it doesn't always work, but it is still worth pursuing and trying.

## Keep Your Goals Clear

Remember, especially in a no-fault state, the law is not on your side. Nothing else matters other than the splitting of finances and child custody, if applicable. You won't get revenge and should not seek it. Don't get caught up in the drama of the divorce, as it will only cause you more stress, be costly and hurt you in the end. You won't be able to out-manipulate a narcissist, especially if they have years of experience, because, for healthy individuals, emotions get in the way.

Don't negatively engage with your spouse. Instead, go into the divorce with focused goals of freedom and stability.

## Therapy is for Therapists

Don't use the attorney as a therapist, for it is more costly than having an actual, qualified therapist. Lawyers will listen to you – and they are great listeners when they want to be –to rack up the paid minutes. Still, you do want to find a sympathetic lawyer. Try to find an attorney specializing in domestic abuse and narcissistic divorces because a divorce with a CNP is a completely different ballgame than most individuals. Most lawyers do not have experience with narcissists in divorces and will not understand the brevity of the situation. They may expect to give your ex the benefit of the doubt or to trust in their word to reach that desired settlement but end up getting manipulated by the CNP in the process.

If you can't find a lawyer specializing in narcissism, make sure your attorney is aware of the problem and proactive. Discuss the patterns of your soon-to-be-ex and the best strategy to deal with them. If your lawyer isn't familiar with this type of personality, be solid in directing the lawyer and set appropriate boundaries. If you hear gaslighting statements such as "it's all in your head" or "nothing can be done," try to find a different lawyer, as it means the CNP can easily manipulate the attorney.

Also, do not confide in mutual friends with the narcissist, especially ones that support and are close to the narcissist. They will be triangulated against you, and some become flying monkeys, doing the CNP's dirty work for them, so there is less blood on the hands of the narcissist. Don't wholly confide in your friends as well. People quickly tire of someone who vents to them as they have their own problems to deal with. Over-sharing can easily damage friendships and can give you a bad reputation. Friends you've trusted may get overwhelmed by too much talk of your divorce, causing a strain in the relationship. Remember, friends are not your therapist either. You can share some details, but nothing too deep. They are not qualified to help you, nor should you expect them to be either. Utilize friends as people to take your mind off the terrible situation instead. After all, friends are for enjoyment.

Lastly, don't share anything about the divorce with your children. Kids are easily manipulated and don't have the best filter. It is also abusive to children when parents burden them with their marital issues. It can lead to the confusion of being stuck between choosing a side, which, as you may remember, becomes parental alienation. Unfortunately, the CNP has no qualms about this behavior. They leave nothing standing in their wake, including the children they use as pawns in their warped game.


## Figure Out the Losing Number

Know what you want and how much you can emotionally and financially withstand because wealthy narcissists will drag the case until you're completely depleted. You must figure out what number you are ready to cut your losses and walk away. There are no wins with CNP divorces. They have been planning the divorce since the day you got married. Leaving a CNP causes serious narcissistic injury, and the level of hatred towards you will be far greater than during the marriage. They truly despise you and will seek to win at all costs. CNPs are professional in their deception and mental illness. It is similar in experience to how seasoned criminals know their craft. They've been practicing and perfecting their manipulations for years.

Unlike a narcissist who has no regretful emotion, your feelings will get in the way. Don't seek revenge. Instead, seek freedom and healing.

## Journal

Journal all the abuse – this is especially helpful in a fault divorce– and start immediately once you realize abuse is occurring. This includes both physical and emotional abuse. It also helps to journal your day anyway for your mental health. By keeping a record of what happened daily, you will have more information at your disposal and feel better prepared. Collect factual evidence on paper and keep screenshots of any electronic communication as well.

It is better to be organized since attorneys have so many clients that they don't easily remember your case from other cases. Therefore, you need to know your case and not rely solely on them. Your lawyer is not your best friend; they care about their well-being above all. No matter how much they say they care about you, their self will come before anything else. Attorneys will typically push for settlement at the end, regardless of whether you want to go to trial, as it is costly, and many attorneys would rather settle than fight in court all day. This is a more beneficial option as trials are quite painful, but you must ensure the settlement is fair. Still, expect it to be unjust as getting any parity in court with a CNP is arduous.

Try to find a good negotiator that can speak the terms with no emotion with the narcissist, stating what you're willing to let go of and what you're not. Utilize the mediators for negotiation purposes. However, the downside of using mediation services is that narcissists can easily manipulate them. Unless you can't afford lawyers, try not to use mediators as your only option. Just as narcissists easily manipulate you and your friends, they will manipulate the mediators, attorneys, and judges. As in the matriphony, the divorce will have the same sway and pull towards the unjust side. Don't expect justice. As much as we are drilled to fight for justice, with CNPs, there is none. Try to get whatever you can get out of them and escape.

## Get Your Freedom

Divorces with a CNP are long and painful. Don't try to get the most out of them, as you will end up with little to nothing. Instead, save money, settle, and start your life over. Try to get as much as you can out of the divorce, but don't let it take years to occur. The longer it takes, the less you end up gaining anyway. Instead, rebuild your life and enjoy your freedom from the CNP ex. After all, narcissists feel a surge of power and control when they control their spouse in a relationship and drag them through the court. They don't care how long the process takes, unlike most who just want it to end. If they don't have you to abuse, they will have to find someone else to fulfill them.

Remember, there aren't any real winners in divorce. Regardless, narcissists often feel they are in it to win. They don't see the point of an equitable split and see themselves as victims. Instead, being proven right is their immediate goal. Therefore, you must have a different goal to avoid going back and forth. Your goal is freedom from the narcissist, and don't give them the satisfaction of dragging out their abuse.

CNPs often try to hoover you back. Going No Contact is vital. Don't answer their texts, phone calls, or meet-up requests. Don't trust their word because they *will* go back on it. They'll say they love you, always loved you, or that you were hard to love, but none of this is true.

Another fitting example of the narcissistic hoover is Netflix's, *The Maid*. The protagonist's husband hoovers her back with false words of care and deceptive support in a challenging time in her life. However, as soon as she was back in his clutches, he began treating her just as awful as before. She lost herself for a time, and it was only until she realized how harmful his behavior towards her was to her daughter did she finally made her escape again.

Some CNPs won't hoover you back, and this is the best outcome you could ever hope of. They may not hoover because the CNP knows you have become wise to their deceit and lies and that nothing will work to entrap or manipulate you again. Consider yourself lucky if they disappear for good. If you have children together, they will move on to them for narcissistic supply in hopes watching your children fall victim to their continued abuse will cause you more anguish. You can't control your children or the CNP. If your children are young adults, it is up to them to decide if they want to continue enduring and putting up with the abusive parent. Hold your boundaries firm and let them know you are there to support them and be there for them. If that means telling your children that you do not wish to hear anything regarding their relationship with their CNP parent that is a perfectly healthy boundary to set for yourself.

You are important and worthy of staying mentally sound, well, and happy. If your child cannot accept that, then that is their choice but not your emotion to absorb. Adult children who care about their parents will not want to bring them more drama and suffering and will respect your boundaries. Those that aren't mature enough will have to learn for themselves, despite it being the hard way. Just like you can't control the CNP, you can't control your adult children. You can, however, educate them on how you are feeling, how they made you feel, and hold your boundaries firm. They will respect you more for it in the long run.

## Avoid Traps

Don't indulge your need for retribution, frustration, or anger with voicemails, emails, or texts that can be construed as threatening or harassment. A CNP will not engage in this direct assault but will try to goad you into it so that you end up looking bad to your lawyer, the judge, and your children. You may not have control over what the CNP does, but you do have control over yourself and how you react to their ploys. Remember, everything they do is to get a reaction from you. Don't let them win by giving them what they desire most.

If the CNP is smearing you to the children, do not engage in that behavior. Your children will come to see the manipulation for what it is, especially since you avoided playing into it. Remain the steady parent there for guidance, love, and stability. Children may not remember what you did but will remember how you made them feel. If you made them feel cared for and safe, whereas the narcissist stressed them out with drama, the children will gravitate towards you. Unfortunately, the CNP's brainwashing and alienation tactics make this exceedingly difficult to achieve with all children. The children who aren't emotionally healthy and not easily swayed will see the truth for what it is.

Sadly, many have lost all their children to a covert narcissistic psychopath as they are constantly groomed from an early age. Explaining this to the court will not bring you any justice either, as it's an uncommonly known mental illness that few understand.

## Research

Read as many books about narcissism as possible, watch YouTube videos, TikToks, and follow Instagram pages about narcissism (mine is @silenceofthenarcs). Watch tv shows such as *The Maid*, *Dirty John*, and *The Undoing*, which do a fantastic job in their portrayal of different narcissistic personality types, especially CNPs.

Another great show to watch is *You*, which takes you into the mind of a dangerous CNP. And, if you can stomach the violence, Squid Game also portrays all the distinct kinds of narcissism, from covert, to overt, to sociopathic and psychopathic.

## Join Support Groups

Find support groups with other people who have had narcissistic relationships and divorces. These groups can be found on social media platforms such as Facebook, Instagram, YouTube, or Meet Up. You may also be able to find local groups in your area as well. Build a safe support system outside anyone who knows and is friends with the narcissist. Long-term friends struggle with grasping the brevity of the situation and won't empathize the way you might hope they would. Friends may withdraw from you, wanting you to move on quicker than you are ready to. Finding people that have been in the same or comparable situation will help prepare and steady you for your bumpy road ahead.

Though divorcing CNPs is difficult and painful, remember you are not alone. There are people who care about you and others who have suffered as you have. Reach out to the healthy people in your life. This was a difficult chapter for me to write as it brought up many traumatic memories, but if it can help just one person, it will be worth it. And now, onto the last and most beautiful chapter, Healing.

# Chapter 8: Healing from Covert Narcissistic Abuse

We have reached the end of the torrential journey of life with a Covert narcissistic psychopath, and now it is time for the final step, which is to heal. No matter how short or long your time was with a CNP, there is still healing to do to recover from the trauma of their manipulation, lies, deceit, and fraud. Healing is never an easy feat to accomplish. And I must admit to you, one never fully heals from such trauma. Healing is truly a life-long journey for all. The moment you stop putting a timeline on your recovery is the moment you will truly begin to get better. One day, you'll be able to look back on those memories and, if they still hurt, know that you did your best to survive a toxic individual. Many do not survive at all, so you have already come out ahead. In the end, you will have grown from the experience, and your emotional maturity will be higher than the CNP's.

As time goes by, you will realize you only lost an unstable, emotionally stunted, abusive person while they lost an emotionally intelligent, empathetic, and caring partner. In the end, though they will never admit it, the CNP play themselves. What is the meaning of life other than to find love and happiness in the short amount of time we get? Every human seeks both in some way, except for CNPs who seek only satisfaction rather than true contentedness.

The first thing you must do to begin the process is to go No Contact with the CNP. Block their number and get a new phone number that you cannot share with the CNP under any circumstances. Remove them from any of your social media sites. You can filter comments on most social media websites to block any comments using a specific word, phrase, or name. This way, if the CNP gets their flying monkeys to make comments under your social media, those comments will not be posted if they match the keywords you block. Also, don't lurk on their social media either. The CNP will post about how great their life is without you on purpose to make themselves look good and stick it to you further. Don't let them have that control over your emotions from a social post. Don't give them the satisfaction of occupying space in your mind anymore. This will be the most challenging task you will undertake as there will be temptations to check in on them to see what they are up to. Know this: if they discarded you or you discarded them, they will have moved on immediately. They cannot be alone. They need constant supply and cannot stand to be alone with themselves.

You will see their new supply and the fake amazing life they live. You'll see posts boasting about how much they give to others and their family, but you know it's not true. It's the same façade they used to capture you. Let them live their heartless life without you allowing them space or time in your already fragile mind. The only way to heal is to go cold turkey: out of sight, out of mind.

Having children with the CNP makes it more difficult to go No Contact, but there are still ways you can protect yourself and maintain distance. CNPs never respect boundaries, so don't try to set boundaries with them. Instead, set healthy boundaries for yourself. Such boundaries you can set are having no communication with the

CNP other than what is required by the court. If you must drop them off and pick them up from the CNP's place, try not to look at the CNP. Don't make any comments to them or gestures. If they try to engage with you, be as passive as you can be.

Be firm about sharing responsibilities. If they want to be a parent, make sure they follow through as one. If they try to push those boundaries, enforce them more, and don't let their excuses hinder or sway your decision. Be organized with your schedule and, if you can, get a signed agreement of the joint custody terms to keep a copy with you to refresh them on their court-ordered responsibilities.

After my divorce, X would try to push boundaries on the little agreed payment he gave for my daughter's expenses which we had agreed to share for an activity she enjoyed and had been doing for years. He wouldn't send her the court-ordered agreed payment on time to invoke a reaction from both her and me. I was No Contact from the beginning of my divorce and onwards, but, in this case, our daughter needed the money.

To get the dud to pay, I had set up a new email specifically for anything divorce-related. It was not used to communicate back and forth, only to send a one-of email informing X to follow through within 48 hours of the email, or I would file with the court that he is in contempt of the divorce decree. I knew there would be issues getting him to pay anything agreed on. As wealthy as he is, he is as cheap as they come.

Try to remember that your kids are watching. Be the mature one the children look up to by offering nothing to the CNP. You don't have to smile or act politely if you don't wish to – though that certainly would annoy the CNP. If there are times when you must cross paths for the kids, try to make the meeting as cordial as possible for your own sake. If you need to hide your reaction, wearing dark sunglasses so the CNP can't see your expression is another way to maintain distance from them while in close proximity.

Another way you can go No Contact is by avoiding places at the time the CNP frequents them. If you have a common social circle with the CNP, try to make new friends outside of that social circle because they end up being flying monkeys for the narcissist. However, if you can't avoid them, never talk about the narcissist with those people. If they bring the CNP up, change the subject or state a firm boundary that you wish not to discuss the CNP. Those who cannot respect that boundary may not be your real friends.

You shift the power from the CNP to yourself when you go No Contact. While the CNP spent years devaluing, disrespecting, and smearing you, you hold the power to do what is best and safest for you. No one has the right to tell you who you are and what you should do or not do in your own life. Their own opinions and perceptions of you are their own. Only you know yourself and what you need most.

Healing from covert, narcissistic, psychopathic abuse is like healing from grief. You must go through each stage of grief to move forward. There is no time limit on how long each stage takes. Only you will know how much time you need. As a reminder, the stages of grief are pain and guilt, anger and bargaining, depression, loneliness, self-reflection, and finally, acceptance. The acceptance phase means accepting things will happen a certain way and that you have no control over them. Expect a painful smear campaign and to be thrown under the bus when the CNP knows you figured them out. They are constantly smearing your name so that when the time comes and you've figured them out, they will already have an alliance behind them, leaving you with no one.

You will have to fight your battle alone for a while because it takes people time to discover the real culprit. By staying out of it and not trying to constantly defend yourself to people, they will realize quickly that you are not the real problem. The toxic individual will never stop smearing you, but people will admire your restraint and maturity if you don't slander them. Eventually, people get sick of hearing about someone's ex and will distance themselves from that person. If you are getting smeared, tell your side of the story only once to those who will genuinely listen. After that, it is up to the person to decide whether they are smart enough to avoid becoming a flying monkey and see you for who you are.

To deal with smearing is to stay as far away from it as possible. Try not to speak to the CNP and ask others not to repeat the CNP's words back to you. Trying to track what they said about you, who they said it to, or defend yourself against their words drives you in maddening circles. You can address the smearing legally, especially if it damages your professional reputation, but don't become overly focused on proving the CNP wrong. If you are in the right, it can still backfire on you. The best thing you can do is to have No Contact with the CNP.

Another thing you must expect is to be replaced quickly by the CNPs. Once they don't have you as a supply source, the CNP will need to find someone else to fulfill their needs. The CNP moving on quickly is not a fault on you, but rather, a fault on them. Eventually, they may discard their new supply and try to hoover you back in, but you must not fall for their love-bombing tactics.

You also need to accept the fact that what you went through was traumatizing. After all, not all devils look evil; some wear a halo and dress in flowing robes. No one else can see the CNP's true evil but you, the direct victim. The horror of being the only one to see the devil is traumatizing. Denying or suppressing your emotions will only cause further harm to yourself in the future. Trauma has a way of creeping up on you no matter what, and it is better that you face it earlier rather than let it surprise you later on.

You may also still feel a fervent connection to the CNP. However, your feelings toward them are not love but unrelenting addiction. This can come out in several ways, such as the Trauma Bond, Cognitive Dissonance, and Stockholm Syndrome in the most extreme situations.


Trauma Bond

The Trauma Bond is the most common result of narcissist abuse. It typically occurs when there is a cycle of abuse or intermittent reinforcement. Intermittent Reinforcement is the most potent manipulation tactic. It occurs when the abuser mixes love-bombing with emotional or physical abuse. The victim is so worn down and starved of affection that the small ounce of love given to them creates a dopamine release. The victim associates this euphoric feeling of relief, though the abuser is the cause of the pain. It's a form of **Breadcrumbing** in which the abuser hurts you emotionally or physically but notices your growing awareness. Therefore, they deflect by throwing "breadcrumbs" of affection, attention, or gifts to reel you back into forgetting the pain, so you believe they are perfect again.

This causes the **Trauma Bond**, which is when the victim desperately hangs onto the hope that the narcissist will change or return to being the person they were in the early love-bombing stage. Most people talk about three trauma responses: fight, flight, or freeze. However, most don't know that there is a fourth trauma response: fawn. The fawn trauma response occurs when the victim tries to please the abuser to avoid being hurt. You try to do anything and everything to make the relationship work, making excuses for the narcissist's behavior in the process. For example, a fawn response is convincing yourself that they were tired that day, or maybe the abuse happened because you didn't finish the laundry, etc.

The fawn response tries to make sense of the abuser's actions to allow the victim to feel safe. By having some logical explanation for the abusive behavior, the victim can justify staying with the narcissist. This was a big one for me as I tried to please X and everyone in my life. I never got what I wished, which was to be loved and appreciated, but I kept trying to please, hoping for the outcome to change. When you try to please others, you become a shadow of yourself. But, when facing rejection, people often try harder to please. The narcissist has conditioned you to act this way, but you will never please them. *You must learn to stop taking on other people's problems, for they are not yours to absorb.* Nothing you do will ever be enough for a CNP, which is not your fault. That is on the narcissist.

Trauma bonds must be broken so that you may heal. The way to recover is to recognize that the narcissist will never change, nor have they ever been that person you thought they were or the person they claim to be. No one is perfect, and we will all hurt each other sometimes, but someone who continuously hurts you is not a good person to be around. The first time someone hurts you could be a mistake. The times after are intentional, especially if you have communicated what the person did hurt you.

People that care about you will stop doing the things that hurt you, but people that don't care will make excuses, false apologies, and false vows to keep stringing you along. Once you realize this, you will discover that you do not need this type of bond. Instead, search for new, healthy bonds with people that will show you the care you deserve.

## Cognitive Dissonance

Cognitive Dissonance is similar to gaslighting in that the CNP says something or acts a certain way and then denies it later, leaving their victim confused and doubting themselves. By definition, it is the disarray a person feels when they simultaneously hold conflicting beliefs about something. For example, the conflicting belief could be whether or not your partner loves you. On the one hand, you believe they love you, but their actions prove otherwise, so you simultaneously feel unloved. This state of confusion keeps victims clinging to the CNP partner though they know they are incapable of loving them. The victim wants to believe their partner loves them, though they know in their hearts that it is simply not true.

One can heal from cognitive dissonance when they receive confirmation of their reality. This can be done through therapy and hearing another unbiased person's opinion on the matter. One can also be made aware of the truth through their journaling. By documenting everything that happened to you, you will be able to see your partner's actions versus their promises. Feeling as though you are loved versus being told you are loved are two vastly different things. You must figure out whether you feel cared about. If you don't, it is time to move on.

Communicating, writing about, and getting therapy for your experience will help you heal from and reduce the cognitive dissonance.

## Stockholm Syndrome

When people think of Stockholm Syndrome, they typically associate it with captors and their prisoners. It's often creepily romanticized in the media with the victim falling in love with their kidnapper or used in horror films with a similar purpose. However, Stockholm Syndrome doesn't only have to occur in captor/prisoner scenarios. It can also occur in narcissistic relationships. It is the most extreme form of bond and requires four elements. The victim is in a life-threatening situation, is isolated, unable to act on survival instincts, and the abuser shows the victim kindness every so often.

Not all narcissists are physically abusive. However, a person can still feel as though their life is being threatened in an emotionally abusive relationship. Most, if not all, narcissists tend to throw violent tantrums and go into a rage when something doesn't go their way. Those receiving such insidious anger can experience fear for their lives or well-being in those situations. As you have also learned, narcissists isolate their victims from those who care about them. When they utilize measures such as financial abuse or threats, a person will feel trapped in the relationship, unable to escape. Lastly, as we know, narcissists drop small bites of false affection to keep their victims addicted to them.

Stockholm Syndrome becomes a survival mechanism in and of itself. When the victim experiences stress and cannot protect themselves, they try to focus on the positive aspects of the situation as the body cannot handle long-term stress. The victim is forced to adapt to new conditions, unideal ones, to survive. Once you sympathize with the abuser, you don't feel like you are a victim anymore, giving you a false sense of control over the situation.

The method of healing from Stockholm Syndrome is to go No Contact with the CNP. Work with an experienced trauma and narcissism specialized therapist to help guide you through the process. Once you take the first step of blocking the narcissist from your life, you will already see a clearer picture. The key to escaping Stockholm syndrome is to focus on the bigger picture rather than the small moments of kindness. Everyone deserves to be treated with kindness and respect. It is not a privilege but a right. When you realize that, you will be able to heal and break that abusive bond with the narcissist.

Journaling helps you realize your right to be treated well. It's easy to say that once you realize it, you will heal, but it's another thing to incorporate it into your life. Just like you have to make time to eat and drink during the day, if you journal your thoughts, ask yourself why you're feeling a certain way, and then answer them, you will discover your inner truth. Deep down, we truly know what is troubling us, and, typically, it is not being cared for, loved, or treated with respect and common decency. As with everything we do in life, the effort we put forth is how much we improve and move through each challenge.

Once you accept who the narcissist truly is and that they never had pure intentions, you will be able to break the traumatic bond that keeps you ensnared in their grasp. As long as you continue to believe and treat the CNP like they are a normal person, you will have difficulty healing. Trying to explain how you feel to a CNP doesn't work. They know what they are doing is wrong; they just don't care. Once you accept this fact and break away from the CNP, you will be able to put what little energy you have left into yourself and start the healing process.

The next step in your journey to recovery is to find ways to help you overcome your past, face your future, and enjoy your present. Naturally, the best method of healing from trauma is therapy. Working with a therapist can help you identify your trauma, work through any conditions you may have due to narcissistic abuse, and guide you through the process at your own pace. Remember, you don't have to face this pain alone.

Make sure to find a therapist with experience in domestic violence, trauma, emotional abuse, and narcissistic abuse. This is no easy task as many therapists have not had the experience or knowledge of dealing with a covert, narcissistic psychopath. Interview or do one appointment with a few therapists and see which one clicks. Many narcissists become therapists as it is just another means to control others and their perceptions while getting paid for it! Still, don't let that dissuade you. Use the knowledge you have learned thus far to find a good match for your needs.

There are also several relatively unknown methods that have been used to help people sort through their trauma. These methods include EMDR and Brain-Spotting. EMDR, or Eye Movement Desensitization and Reprocessing, utilizes eye movements to help you target different memories. Memories with negative feelings associated with them can be viewed from a new insight, one of your own makings. It is not so much the therapist that changes your point of view but your intellectual and emotional processes that allow you to recall a traumatic memory and allow yourself to feel empowered by it rather than stunted. The wounds don't simply close but transform into something new entirely.

Brain-Spotting is similar in that you associate different spots that your eyes focus on with a feeling. Then, you connect those spots. Suppose one spot is a traumatic memory or negative feeling, whereas another spot is a joyful memory or positive feeling. In that case, the person goes back and forth between those spots until the negative feeling is reduced. The eye positions or Brainspots indicate where trauma, anxiety, depression, or other issues occur in the brain, allowing them to be fully processed.

Other methods of therapy include hypnotherapy, individual counseling, and group therapy. The goal is to try out all the various options to see what works best for you and your trauma.

Healing does not have to only occur in therapy, nor should it. There are many ways you can take control of your process. The more reading you do about Narcissistic Personality Disorder, Covert Narcissism, Covert Psychopathic Narcissism, and emotional abuse, the more tools you will have in your arsenal to protect yourself from further harm. After all, therapy can also be expensive. I have found that putting the work in to learn about this psychological plague is helpful to healing as well. The more you learn about it, the more you realize how real it is and how many people are affected by narcissistic abuse.

You can join online support groups to learn about others with similar stories and discover that you aren't alone. Being an active or participatory member of those support groups will also help you stay on track with your goals and prevent you from falling back into the schemes of your narcissistic ex. What you can learn from others is just as important as what you can learn on your own.

Another excellent way to heal is to try out new hobbies. Spending time with loving animals, such as a dog, for instance, can do wonders to boost your oxytocin (happiness). Unconditional love from an animal is sometimes exactly what you need after a relationship, where love is rarely given. You can also increase your oxytocin levels by spending time with friends who care about you in easygoing, fun settings.

The feeling of dopamine or adrenaline from the rush of being in a narcissistically abusive relationship can also be replaced by much healthier alternatives. Try out different activities that bring you a thrill, such as rock climbing, biking, walking, horseback riding, a thrill ride at an amusement park, or meeting new people for the first time in an unfamiliar environment. Anything that brings you a sense of fear or anticipation with positive consequences is fair game. However, make sure not to force yourself into anything you aren't ready for.

I started slow due to challenges with my health from years of abuse and my autoimmune-related challenges. I went for walks and didn't set overly ambitious goals like my old self would have done. A short walk did as much good as a longer one. I let go of intrusive thoughts on my walks by focusing on my surroundings. By looking at the beautiful clouds in the sky, the birds in the trees or those that flew above me, the grass, plants, flowers, and the thousands of tiny ants traveling in rows between each concrete seam.

Still, with all the surrounding beauty, a traumatic or triggering memory would sneak in. This happens because your brain is programmed to remember pain more easily than bliss. For instance, my last walk with X and my two children was a terribly negative experience. Of course, that would enter my brain just as I'm enjoying my walk because it's almost like a defensive mechanism. Our hippocampus shrinks as we endure years of abuse and trauma. You have to build that part of your brain with more positive memories. However, the mind wanders; if not fully built back up, it will happen more often than you wish.

You will have waves of ups and downs, but guess what? You have the power to control those intrusive thoughts. You can choose to dwell on it or refocus on those who brought you joy. I would catch myself, and in my head, I would tell myself to stop, appreciate the beauty around me, and don't allow that pain to ruin the moment. I'd then take several deep breaths. No matter how sick you may be of hearing it, deep breathing works.

You don't have to do many breathes, but if you are feeling anxious or sad, take full, deep belly breathes of counts of four to seven in through your nose and then four to seven counts of slowly blowing it out of your mouth. Repeat until the negative feelings disappear, and you begin to refocus on what brought you joy.

Like anything in life, practice makes perfect. You can't just talk about doing it; you must make yourself do it and not just sporadically here and there but on schedule and often. You must schedule it because if you don't schedule that time for it, it won't happen. I am of this nature as well. I must make time for it or regress into my bad habits of allowing the triggering, intrusive thoughts to take hold. It takes doing an activity for sixty or more consecutive days to form a good habit. Map it out, schedule it and repeat it until you have it down. Remember, this is to improve your well-being and rebuild and preserve your happiness, health, and prosperity.

It is time to focus on yourself and do what makes you happy. Don't be afraid to try something new and fail! The fact you went out and tried is what matters the most. The most important part is to enjoy whatever new ventures you embark on. Spoil yourself now and then with things you want, not just things you need. Maybe you want some new clothes or accessories. Or maybe you want to try that new restaurant that just opened. Try to make your new life unpredictable and find a different activity to try out every day!

If you are financially drained, you can still do things for yourself that cost next or nothing at all. Walking, going to the park, or visiting a dog park. If you don't have a dog, you can still enjoy the company of others and their pets. I often went to a local barn to visit the horses and ponies. They brought me such joy and therapy I cannot begin to describe. If you love birds, you can go bird-watching on nature trails. The options are endless if you take the opportunity to try incorporating something new into your daily routine.

You can also find hobbies that reduce stress and allow you to remain calm and at peace. Try to find exercises or activities that allow you to be mindful such as yoga or journaling. You can also set a reading goal for the month or year of how many books you wish to get through, whether it be reading for pleasure or learning. Other activities that help me wind down include crocheting, sewing, creating artwork, writing, and sitting down to watch a feel-good movie or show.

While all these methods make your days more enjoyable, you still need to put in the emotional work. Don't use new hobbies as a distraction but as a supplement to your emotional healing. Allow yourself to feel all the emotions you need to feel. If you're angry, settle into that anger; don't push it away. You have a right to be angry, and by embracing it, you will be more likely to stand up for yourself in the future.

With anger comes sadness. As people, we typically try to avoid sadness at all costs. But, allowing yourself to have a good cry and the sadness to wash over you is healthy. It does not make you weak. Crying makes you human. Ironically, you can still feel sad when you start to get better. This is because you will realize what you missed out on and how badly certain people failed you. You will realize what the younger you deserved versus what the toxic individuals in your life made you feel you deserved. Allow yourself the time to grieve and the space to feel that grief. The end of a narcissistic relationship can feel just as painful as losing someone close to you. In a way, the person you fell in love with died, for you will not see that person again. It is okay to mourn the loss of the person you were tricked into believing they were and the person you once were before being with the narcissist.

Something that is uncommonly discussed is how being with a CNP can cause physical illness. Prolonged, chronic stress from an emotionally or psychologically abusive relationship wreaks havoc on the mind and the body. The body's stress response is self-limiting; everything turns back to normal once the perceived threat is gone. However, if you are living in a situation where you constantly feel like you are walking on eggshells, your body becomes trapped in fight, flight, freeze, or fawn responses. These recurrent stress responses and overexposure to cortisol can cause illnesses such as anxiety, depression, digestive issues, headaches, muscle tension and pain, heart ailments, high blood pressure, strokes, sleep problems, weight gain, memory loss, and concentration troubles. Modern medicine can do little against the chronic plague of a CNP. Once again, the only solution to this issue is to go No Contact.

Another part of healing is to speak up. The CNP silenced you for so long, but now, you are free to tell your story when you feel ready. Whether through sharing in a support group, writing an article or creative nonfiction piece about your experience, contributing to a discussion board, or telling friends and family about what you went through, let your voice be heard. However, it is necessary to filter who you share with and make certain they are emotionally mature and in a safe, supportive environment. Everyone will have opinions, and it's okay for them to express them and have indifference. Don't allow others' opinions to become yours unless you feel they fit within your ideals. For so long, we did for others and failed to put ourselves first. It's perfectly fine to respect yourself. Many will not respect your boundaries until you let them know how you wish to be treated. If they cannot treat you as you'd treat them, they are not worth having in your life.

Lastly, I believe you need not forgive the narcissist to move on. The best way to heal is to forgive yourself. There is no way you could have known what you were getting into when you first started a relationship with a CNP. If you had known, you would have run in the other direction and never looked back. But you were fooled, tricked, love bombed, idealized, controlled, manipulated, devalued, and isolated by the CNP. People might ask, what about taking responsibility for your part too? Of course, you must reevaluate your choices to learn from them and not repeat those same mistakes. Red flags don't always appear red until after you learn about them. You can hold yourself accountable for what you missed, but you can't blame or resent yourself for not knowing. None of us wanted to lose everything and have to start our life over.

We are survivors, and we will continue to push forward.

# Afterword

Thank you, dear reader, for reading my story. Writing this book has been both painful and therapeutic, but I am so grateful to have the opportunity to share my truth and help others who may be going through a similar experience.

While my book is an introduction to life with a Covert Narcissistic Psychopath, there are far more essential resources you must continue researching and learning about. I recommend you dive into other books, videos, websites, social media support groups, articles, etc. You can never learn too much information, and each resource offers new findings and knowledge that will strengthen you. Knowledge is truly empowering and healing. I wish I had more during my life, but it was not as exposed as it is now. Here are some of my favorite resources that helped me through my healing process.

**Terms to research and study as CNP's have more than one personality disorder:**

Narcissistic Personality Disorder (NPD)
Borderline Personality Disorder (BPD)
Anti-Social Personality Disorder (ASPD)
Dissociative Identity Disorder (DID)
Cluster B Personality Disorders
Covert Narcissist
Sociopath

Psychopath

Narcissist

Narcopath

Hidden Abuse

Coercive Control

Emotional Abuse

Psychological Manipulation

Psychological Abuse

Emotional Incest

Parental Alienation

Financial Abuse

Emotional Vampire

Emotional Rape

Covert Abuse

Domestic Violence

Domestic Abuse

Child Abuse

Pathological Liar

Compulsive Liar

Toxic Abuser

Toxic Relationships

Covert Manipulation

YouTubers and Websites that have brought valuable information to me (I don't personally endorse any of these sites, and this is information that I found helpful in my learning journey during my healing process):

**The Little Shaman**

Littleshaman.org


**Healing After the Narcissist – Linda Martinez-Lewi, Ph.D., LMFT**

Thenarcissistinyourlife.com


**Surviving Narcissism – Dr. Les Carter**

Survivingnarcissism.tv

Drlescarter.com


**Debbie Mirza**

Debbiemirza.com


**Michele Lee Nieves Coaching**

Micheleleenieves.mykajabi.com


**Angie Atkinson**

Queenbeeing.com


**Melanie Tonia Evans**

Meanietoniaevans.com

Youcanthrivebook.com

## Books I have found helpful:

The Covert Passive-Aggressive Narcissist – Debbie Mirza

Power: Surviving & Thriving After Narcissistic Abuse – Shahida Arabi

Psychopath Free – Jackson MacKenzie

The Covert Passive-Aggressive Narcissist – Debbie Mirza

Without Conscience: The Disturbing World of the Psychopaths Among Us – Robert D. Hare

In Sheep's Clothing – George Simon, JR., Ph.D.

Dangerous Liaisons: How to Recognize and Escape from Psychopathic Seduction – Claudia Moscovici

Husband, Liar, Sociopath – O.N. WARD

Splitting – Bill Eddy and Randi Kreger

Healing from Hidden Abuse – Shannon Thomas, LCSW

The Sociopath Next Door – Martha Stout

How To Spot A Dangerous Man Before You Get Involved – Sandra L. Brown, MA

Breaking Free – Lisette SQ

Complex PTSD: From Surviving to Thriving – Pete Walker

Will I ever Be Free of You – Karyl McBride, Ph.D.

The Gift Of Fear – Gavin De Becker

The Body Remembers – Babette Rothschild

Empath: A Complete Guide for Developing Your Gift and Finding Your Sense of Self – Judy Dyer

DSM-5-TR – Diagnostic and Statistical Manual of Mental Disorders – American Psychiatric Association – Technical read for those that want to dive in further.

If you are still questioning whether you are in a toxic or narcissistically abusive relationship, the following few pages have a quiz that may help you gain some clarity on your situation. While the quiz cannot diagnose anyone with Narcissistic Personality Disorder nor solidly define your relationship, it may be able to help you make sense of your doubts and questions.

## ARE YOU A COVERT NARCISSIST QUIZ by SCOTT BARRY KAUFMAN

Take the quiz below: 1= untrue, 2= uncharacteristic, 3= neutral, 4= true, characteristic and 5= very true, strongly agree. Assign a number from 1-5 of how each question relates to you. Add the final numbers up, and if you score 87 points and above – you are a Covert Narcissist (The test only works if you are honest with your answers)

1. I can become entirely absorbed in thinking about my personal affairs, health, care, or relationships with others.

2. My feelings are easily hurt by ridicule or the slighting remarks of others.

3. When I enter a room, I often become self-conscious and feel that the eyes of others are upon me.

4. I dislike sharing the credit of achievement with others.

5. I feel that I have enough on my hand without worrying about other people's troubles.

6. I feel that I am temperamentally different from most people.

7. I often interpret the remarks of others in a personal way.

8. I easily become wrapped up in my own interests and forget the existence of others.

9. I dislike being with a group unless I know I'm appreciated by at least one of those present.

10. I am secretly "put out" or annoyed when other people come to me with their troubles, asking me for time and sympathy.

11. I am jealous of good-looking people.

12. I tend to feel humiliated when criticized.

13. I wonder why other people aren't more appreciative of my good qualities.

14. I tend to see other people as being either great or terrible.

15. I sometimes have fantasies about being violent without knowing why.

16. I am especially sensitive to success and failure.

17. I have problems that nobody else seems to understand.

18. I try to avoid rejection at all costs.

19. My secret thoughts, feelings, and actions would horrify some of my friends.

20. I tend to become involved in relationships in which I alternately adore and despise the other person.

21. In a group of friends, I often feel very alone.

22. I resent others who have what I lack.

23. Defeat or disappointment usually shame or anger me, but I try not to show it.

# Acknowledgments

Thank you to everyone who helped me bring this book to life: my dear friend, who read and commented on the manuscript, my editor for their time and input, and the survivors who found this book in their hands who read and brought awareness and light to the years of suffering in silence. Never let anyone treat you so poorly again. Your spirit and life matter.

**#NOCONTACT**

**@silenceofthenarcs**

**silence of the narcs**

# About The Author

Motivated by personal experience with a Covert Narcissistic Psychopath and many Malignant Narcissists, a survivor of Domestic Violence and unrelenting health challenges with a passion and drive to shed light and awareness on scoundrels that prey, harm, and impact the lives of trusting, kind souls. Silence of the Narcs' mission is to give survivors the knowledge to find their voice, a safe place, and a means to validate, share, and learn from their experiences.

**#NOCONTACT**

**@silenceofthenarcs**

**silence of the narcs**

Printed in Great Britain
by Amazon

86840376R00139